Introduction

Having lived some of his childhood in Kilbeggan, County Westmeath, Robert moved to Tallaght in his early years and lived at the foothills of the Dublin Mountains. It was in these hills that he spent a large amount of his youth, on his grandad's farm, under the influence of his four uncles. Considering the lush valley of Glenasmole is only five miles from the ever-growing town, Robert was quite happy juggling the two totally different ways of rural and urban life.

When not on the farm he was like any other teenager, living in Tallaght and getting involved with the local GAA club, among others. Being a typical teen, he found ample opportunity to hang out with his gang of mates and get up to all sorts of mischief; but overnight Robert's life changed forever, after a terrible car accident.

Among other horrific injuries he was left permanently blind.

More than two decades on, and having achieved several huge goals that many fully-sighted people would not dare to even take on, he finally tells his story in the pages of this book.

It's an autobiography that is shockingly hard-hitting and brutally honest – an emotional roller coaster that will have you crying one moment and laughing the next. But it is also incredibly uplifting.

This story, is told by a man who, for eighteen years, could see perfectly – before he was plunged into the depths of despair. But it is not just about how he turned his life around. This book goes further than that.

This book goes, beyond the darkness...

Acknowledgements

I would like to thank Eileen Casey, because if it wasn't for her inspiring tuition in her creative writing class, this book would never have begun.

My extreme gratitude goes to Sheila McMillan, for the countless hours she spent reading my initial draft.

There are those of you that are mentioned in the pages of this book that I am eternally grateful to, because you reached out to me in my time of need and helped me in the early challenges of my blindness. You continue to be there for me today.

When reading this book I would like you to spare a thought and a prayer for the big man, Eamon, who I fondly mention in this book. His health is not great; may he recover soon.

To those who sent me photographs, including Theo Finnegan – my best ever drinking buddy and worst ever tandem pilot. And to Derek O'Reilly who was always there when called upon – my friendly shadow. Also to Brenda Cross who came to my rescue with photos from Kilimanjaro.

Also to my tremendous pal Mike Knightson – I never realised what a close friend I really had in him, until recently.

These are just some of the people I am eternally grateful to – as the saying goes *Lovers come and go but friends* [and I mean real friends] *stay forever*. It was you lot who helped me see through the darkness and beyond.

Finally, I would like to give warm thanks to my publisher, Emer Cleary, of Emu Ink. Without her passion, skill and expertise, this book would not exist.

Dedication

I would like to dedicate this book to those who face adversity, challenge it, and beat it every day of their lives.

Also to Sheila, whose endless courage in battling and beating her Cancer is an inspiration.

And finally to my cousin, Elaine, who taught me how to accept and enjoy life for what it truly is – a gift.

Beyond
the Darkness

by
Robert Dowdall

June 2014

Beyond the Darkness

2014

Published by Emu Ink Ltd
www.emuink.ie

Cover design by Gwen Taylour

ISBN: 978-1-909684-46-1

Chapter One

I CAN still visualise that night – the one that changed my life forever.

The, now haunting, lyrics of Freddie Mercury's *I Want It All* blasting through the stereo speakers as myself and Dermot sang along with gusto – and the car sped towards the Dublin mountains – oblivious to the thick descending fog that awaited us.

We were in flying form as we navigated the back roads down over Ballinascorney, at my suggestion.

"Do you think you will pull with your one tonight?" I had asked earlier, in the toilets of the pub.

"Not a chance in hell," he'd laughed. "Sure they're too bleeding sober!"

"True," I'd relented. "But if you had a chance, which one would you go for?"

His answer pissed me off greatly – it being the same girl I was hoping to score with.

"All right," I'd said. "We'll have a wager to see who pulls her." And without even washing our hands we shook on it.

"What do you think of going the back road home and stopping on the top of Ballinascorney hill?" I then asked.

"For bleeding what?"

"So we can look at the light over the city."

"Are you mad or what?"

A bit slow on the uptake was Dermot, but when he saw my smirk he soon copped what I was up to.

"Jesus, Bob, that's not a bad idea," he'd grinned.

"Sure if nothing else Locko, it's a nice view."

We would never get to see those lights though, not then and, for me, not ever again.

Neither I, nor Dermot, pulled that night or even got to chance our arm. The furthest we got was a sharp bend in the road known as Doolin's Corner. There, on that corner, Queen, and Freddie's magnificent voice, suddenly died – as did so much more.

To this day I don't recall the impact and maybe I should be grateful. The night, in fact, was a total wipeout from the time we left the pub to the time I briefly came around as I was being rushed to hospital by ambulance. It's amazing, though, the memories that come flooding back as I sit here writing.

I remember the sirens blaring away and Dermot requesting they be turned off because they were "giving him a pounding headache," as the two girls cried beside us.

I was in and out of consciousness all night and will forever be haunted by my coming around to find my devastated parents by my bedside. There was a lot of commotion and I didn't know what was happening – all I knew was that I was wrapped up in what seemed to be tinfoil.

Frightened, I asked what was going on and it was my mom's voice that reached out to me.

"You are in hospital and the tinfoil wrapped around your body is for shock."

All I could think of, to say in return, was, "I'm sorry."

I did not realise it then, but my mother was the rock of strength that reached through the darkness that night and her voice, and aura, told me I would get through whatever lay in store for me. My image of Atlas carrying the world on his shoulders is somewhat distorted because in my experience, and this is where it started, it's women who carry the crushing load.

I was very much conscious when the medical staff became concerned that I might have internal bleeding. The procedure for this was excruciating as I had to receive a stomach puncture before a tube was directed into me, to enable doctors to determine if this was the case. I don't know if I was really aware of the extent of my injuries, or if it is a mechanism of the mind to shut down in order to enable the body to cope. Whatever the case, I only became aware of how serious the situation was the following morning.

Once again I came around, but this time it was to hear a priest praying beside me.

"Deeermoooottttttt!" I screamed at the top of my lungs – devastated as I immediately assumed something had happened to my best friend.

But again my mother's voice reached out to me and told me he was fine.

It was only then the realisation dawned on me. The priest was praying for me.

As I was wheeled down to theatre soon after I honestly felt I was going to die, and just before I was put under anesthetic I asked one of the medical staff what was happening.

"We're about to operate to save your eyes," came the reply.

Chapter Two

MY operation was over seven hours long and because of the length of time under anesthetic my body went into extreme spasm, leaving it necessary for me to be sedated again.

When I finally came around my parents were, once again, by my bedside.

"You're finally awake," my mother remarked gently. "You have been out of it for some time."

"How long?" I asked, amazed and somewhat puzzled to be informed that I was in and out of consciousness for almost two days.

"You have been through a major operation and your face and eyes are covered in bandages," she almost whispered.

"How bad do I look?"

"What does that matter? You're lucky to be alive."

I was too afraid to ask her anything else so while she and my dad hovered over me for the next hour or so, we just made small talk.

My first recollection of registering that Dermot was alright was later that same night.

"Bob, are you awake?" came his voice.

"That you, Locko?"

"Have you bandages and shit over your eyes and face?" He sounded shocked.

"Yep. It's bleeding poxy. I can't see shit. Mind you, don't think I would want to, the smells are bad enough."

"Did you eat any of that shite they were dishing out tonight?

"Fuck no, sure I almost puked from the smell of it. Could you eat it?"

"Nah, my old man brought me in a burger and chips."

"You jammy bastard, why didn't I think of that?" I knew, though, that I couldn't have eaten a burger even if I was presented with it, but that didn't matter.

"Have you a headache? he asked.

"Pounding," I replied.

This small talk went on through the night and in our innocence I think we were both trying to reassure one another, but were too afraid to mention what was really going on. I cannot recollect much more of anything in the eleven days I spent in hospital after the accident, but what does stand out in my mind, quite vividly, are the initial reactions of my family and friends on first meeting me.

If anything, I saw all of them, the first time, stripped down to their very soul. It was a revelation to witness people who I had down as being tough as nails, collapse, and others, whom I had thought shy and vulnerable, prove themselves to be anything but.

My big sis, Loreena, I had in the tough as nails category – cut from the same cloth as my mother – and, true to form, she bounded into the room and simply remarked, "Jaysus, who dragged you through the ditch backwards?"

She was the first one to get any sort of reaction out of me. What could I do but laugh through my swollen and battered face?

On noticing my discomfort in trying to laugh, however, my mother rebuked her on her comment, and it made me laugh even more when Loreena turned to Locko and told him he didn't look any different – he still looked as terrible as always.

It was some time later I was to find out that after the brave front she had put on for my benefit, she went outside and poured her broken heart out.

*

"Can you see how many fingers I am holding up?" asked the young male intern.

"No," was my solemn reply.

It was the first morning the bandages were removed from my eyes and the difficulty I had just trying to open them was immense, with the swelling so incredible, and surrounding tissue and muscle so extremely weakened. I had been told not to expect much from that first operation, its main purpose being to remove the glass from my eyes, but what followed was the news that in those initial stages my eyes appeared too damaged and weakened to perform any sight-saving surgery. It was another devastating blow, but to put into context just how weak my body was in those first few days, and how unable I was for any more crushing revelations, would be to recollect the fact that I was totally oblivious to the young nurse whose duty it was to give me a bed bath every morning.

*

The month that followed my first operation, and the wait for my second and decisive one, was excruciating. I believe that everyone I know was silently praying for a miracle and the amount of Mass cards I received was countless. I always assumed that mass cards where only given to the families of those poor unfortunates that died, so this kindly gesture from well wishers unfortunately gave me not the intended comfort, but more the shivers, and a deep sense of foreboding. Looking back on that month, while I waited for the operation that would seal my fate, it seems so surreal – like I wasn't really living in my body or actually present in the moment. People hovered around me in confused silence, saying plenty but at the same time saying nothing at all, really. I wonder now, what confused thoughts floated around in their heads or were they, like me, numbed – too afraid to think?

December 8th, 1989, was the day scheduled for my last operation, a date that is indelibly printed in my mind – not just for the obvious reason, but because my mother reminded me continuously that it was the day of the immaculate conception of the Virgin Mary. I remember, whilst I was in theatre, she spent the whole time in the little chapel of the hospital praying for some sort of intervention.

And, later, as the bandages came off once more a young student doctor shone a light into my eyes and all of a sudden a slight miracle occurred.

I could make out the light that was incredibly bright. Initially I wondered if the guy was *trying* to blind me, but within seconds when he, once again, asked how many fingers he was holding up my instant delight disintegrated.

I could see nothing but a mere shadow.

"Sure how the hell could he see anything with the room practically pitch black and the doctor himself black?" remarked a rather annoyed guy beside me, and it was that Dublin wit that gave us all the tension relief we so desperately needed right then.

The days that followed in hospital were spent entirely in the unbelievably uncomfortable position of lying prone – that's face down on my stomach. Now you may think, sure what is the problem in that? But trust me, when you have to do it for ten days, around the clock, with severe stomach pain, it's a nightmare. The stomach puncture that was performed on me on the night of my accident had severely weakened the lining around the wall of my stomach and the steroids I was on, to try and strengthen my eyes, only added to this dilemma.

The peculiar reason for having me lie in such an uncomfortable position was that my eyes were so badly torn, and the retina so scarred, that there was a large amount of micro stitches strategically placed at the back of my eyes – trying to patch them into some sort of corrective state. I had to lie facedown because there was a gas bubble put into the back of my eyes, the pressure from which was holding everything in place. Christ, isn't the miracle of science a wondrous thing? It continues to baffle me how the hell they can perform such amazing and delicate procedures – my simple explanation of which certainly does not do it any justice.

Unfortunately though, miracle or science, none of them worked for me. Whatever happened or didn't happen, it all went terribly wrong and as the days progressed even the little light I was initially granted began to fade.

Chapter Three

WHEN operations fail and something goes tragically wrong, loved ones seek answers. And when there are none to be found they submit to a simplistic faith in their belief that it was God's decision… Or they take the other notion that it was the doctor's fault and he messed up in theatre by "trying to play God."

We also have a great saying that "God never gives us a cross we can't carry," and, around this time, if I heard this once, from people with a daft sense of faith or simply with nothing better to say, I heard it a million times.

What a crock of shit? I thought then and still think now. Whatever about a lack of divine intervention, I know, without a shadow of a doubt, that my surgeon did his very best to save my eyes and while my mother prayed to God I left it in his capable hands.

It just wasn't meant to be.

*

In the aftermath of the tragedy there is one day in particular that, looking back, was hilarious but also a valuable lesson in my early days of darkness.

I was walking down the corridor of the hospital, precariously linked to my mother's arm, with Dermot at my other side; when I opened my big mouth to berate the head matron of my ward.

"She is a cantankerous bitch," I remarked to my mother.

"That's not nice," mom replied. "Sure she has a damn hard job to do putting up with you two."

"But you should hear the way she talks to the junior nurses," I ranted on. "She is nothing but a bloody cow."

Just then I heard Locko cough, but I thought nothing of it.

"Hey, Locko, you tell my mother what that old bitch is like," I continued. Another cough.

"Well?" I persisted, oblivious to the stiffening of my mother's arm.

"I am taking the fifth on this one," Locko answered, suspiciously.

"You bollix," I said. "Sure only the other day you said…"

Suddenly a piercing pain shot through my arm – the work of a pinch.

"Arrrghhh!!" My scream echoed through the corridor.

"That's quite enough," my mother declared.

My pride smarting, however, I ignored her rebuke and was just about to continue my abusive rant, when it suddenly dawned on me that Dermot was now walking behind, and not alongside, of me. Then came the unmistakable voice of the matron speaking in her sweetest tone and I felt my face grow pale.

"Now, Robert, sure I am not all that bad. Don't I keep the girls on their toes, stopping them from flirting with you? And every day I greet you with the sweetest smile you can imagine."

I was lost for words – too embarrassed to say anything and it wasn't lost on her. I could tell she was enjoying my discomfort as she leaned in towards me and planted a big kiss on my cheek.

"Now that will teach you to open your big mouth again," my mother laughed while shoving me by the arm down the corridor, like a bold child.

From that day forward the matron and I actually got on quite well and I learned a valuable lesson – if you have nothing good to say about someone then don't say anything at all… or if you do at least make sure they are not around!

In general, and as a result of that particular incident I think, these days if I have something to say to someone I make sure I say it to their face. A lot of people regard me as being extremely direct and blunt – but hey, that is the way I expect people to be with me.

Chapter Four

AFTER my last operation it more or less became an annoying and frustrating waiting game. Every fortnight I would begrudgingly travel with my parents to the hospital where the doctor would examine me to determine if there was any progress with the development of my retina and optic nerve. By that stage my eyes were so weakened that my eyelids were constantly shut so the doctor had to pry them open when shining the light into them.
Again I could make out the light – but damn all else.

As the weeks slowly progressed, though, my eyes gradually became stronger and the night they opened voluntarily I was ecstatic – if only briefly.

I was at a friend's party with my sister. It was New Year's night and on seeing my eyes open for the first time in months my big sis shed tears of euphoria. It was not innocence that prompted her to ask the question but agonising hope, and so half afraid but half excited, she ventured, "Well, what can you see?"

I was happy that I could now open my eyes but I did not want to dampen her spirits, so when I replied I exaggerated the fact that I could see a bright light and make out the odd shadow. In truth, the light I could see was nothing compared to what I described but my sister's reply cheered me up more than the incident itself, when she replied, "Sure that's a start anyway."

Loreena and I were always extremely close, especially in our early childhood days while living in Kilbeggan County Westmeath. Back then, armed with a profound innocence that was easy to obtain and sustain, considering the environment in which we grew up in, our early years of childhood were bliss.

Before my younger sister came along, Loreena and I only had each other and the vast wilderness of our back yard with surrounding fields provided a magical world where the possibilities were endless. As a tomboy my sister was great company for me, never indulging in girly games but preferring, instead, to play Cowboys and Indians; where the cowboy was always the underdog and we both fought to be great warrior chiefs.

We never had Great War parties, but spent most of the time trying to sit crossed-legged puffing on our peace pipes, made of branches and twigs. In our imaginations we even created a wonderland of fantasy from the sky.

We would forever lie on the grass and create shapes out of the clouds. I remember vividly the day we ran screaming and yelling, seeking out our parent's protection, as "The Devil" made his way from the sky to get us.

For days after we were scared to look up into those clouds.

During the migration of the many flocks of birds, we always imagined that the leading bird was the headmaster and the rest his pupils. The last one, which we waited patiently for to fly by, was the straggler – the bold and mischievous one of the class.

I can't ever remember Loreena not been there for me – even in our early years of moving to Dublin. At seven years of age, it was a huge transition moving from the country to what I then regarded as a major city; and I found it quite hard to adapt, were she just seemed to fit in.

I was a constant target for bullies during those early years, in Tallaght. The older kids nicknamed me *Bob the Babe*, as I never stood up for myself and if picked upon I would go running with my tail between my legs, seeking my sister's protection.

There was a boy next door who was a year or two older than me and at almost every opportunity he would pick a fight with me. Loreena, however, would always come to my rescue and, amazingly, with what seemed like no effort at all, beat the crap out of him. She soon achieved a reputation as a good fighter and gained the respect of even the tougher heads on the estate. She could have taken all the girls on the estate and many of the guys came to fear her as well.

A few years later she became even more feared throughout the neighbourhood as she gained an ally in her Jack Russell, Jackie. The two became a force to be reckoned with – my sister fighting like a mule as her dog took sizeable lumps out of her opponents' legs... or so the story goes.

Now I am not trying to make any comparisons between my sis and the Incredible Hulk, but this fictional hero became an obsession for me around this time. Not that Loreena mutated into a green giant with muscles rippling out of her body from head to toe, but she did, sort of, transform into a mean fighting figure when angered. In Bill Bixby, the actor who mutated into the Incredible Hulk, however, I saw myself.

Bill seemed quite defenceless in the world and I identified with that. He was thin and seriously shy, but most of all he was a constant target for brutes who picked on him, and I could certainly relate to that.

For me, at that time, it was wonderful to see that at the end of each show the weaker guy would win by miraculously mutating into the Hulk and beating the shit out of the bullies and bad guys.

I secretly longed for my frail, thin body to somehow transform into a tower of green muscle and beat the crap out of my next door neighbour – but I had to make do with my fearsome sister and the fierce hound of Tallaght.

And I may never have become the Incredible Hulk, but everyone has a limit and mine was eventually reached.

It was a pleasurable and most memorable day when, finally, the giant that *was* growing inside of me could take it no more and emerged with such a fury that I surprised everyone, not least myself.

It was a glorious day and the green in front of my house was filled with children of all ages – from little toddlers, to teenagers and the odd adult availing of the afternoon sun. I was playing a game called Kerbs with, probably my only friend at the time, Derek, and as the game was progressing, the bully, who shall remain nameless, suddenly grabbed the ball and started to taunt us, but mostly me.

On realising I was not going to challenge him for the ball and when his name-calling became tiresome, even to him, he unexpectedly let the ball fly and it hit me full force in the face.

I was in shock. Shock and pain, but rather than the usual tears choking me up all I sensed was an incredible rage – one that had been simmering for some time – burst forth and spew out of me.

The acid that had been tearing into my gut for so long, thanks to his constant harassment, had turned to bile, which was boiling inside of me – and the time had come to poison him with it.

Before he, or me for that matter, was aware of it I was on top of him, beating the living daylights out of him. I honestly don't know how long I was pounding; all my energy from the frustration, rage and humiliation that I had suffered at his hands, was now going into pummelling him. All I know is that before a concerning adult could get to his rescue and manage to pull me off, he had received tenfold of anything he had ever given to me.

The sheer terror and fear I saw in his eyes, as I was being pulled off him, was a joy to behold and it gave way to a turning point for me.

I was, never again, called *Bob the Babe*... at least not within earshot anyway.

Chapter Five

I HAD a fantastic home life, between Kilbeggan and Dublin, but not all of my childhood was pleasant. My early years in school, for example, were anything but. On my first day at school I could not understand why I could not be in the same class as my sister, as up until then we were practically inseparable. I was upset and my voice could be heard throughout the school as I demanded to be put in the same class as her. When I finally realised this was not going to happen I tried with extreme effort, but in vain, to run away and back to the familiar surrounds and sanctuary of my home.

My first school was run by the nuns and I have no hesitation in stating that my first teacher was a right bitch. I had a few encounters with her as a child of only four and one of the main reasons for her disdain of me was the fact that I am left handed. To the twisted, demented mind of this nun, it was not a legitimate way to approach writing and anyone who did was regarded as lazy, slow or even corrupted by some evil entity.

So this nun was determined to rid me of my terrible infliction, as she saw it, and made it her holy calling to beat me with a leather strap across the knuckles every time she caught me writing with my left hand. I can safely say that some of my childhood innocence disappeared thanks to that sad and sorry nun and because of her my image of school, and all it had to offer, became somewhat distorted. To me it was a place of punishment and I disliked everything it stood for. I was regarded as different and slow and I soon believed that to be the case.

*

Sadly things did not change much for me in primary school when I moved to Dublin, either. The perpetrator of my hell was most definitely a she-devil and, though not a nun, I reckon was as sad and frustrated as the previous one that had taught me in Kilbeggan. Again she assumed I was slow and she frequently declared this to the rest of the class. When not satisfied with the reaction she would literally shake me into believing it, by grabbing both my arms and repeating her bitter and twisted words over and over like a mantra. Looking back now I find it somewhat odd and peculiar that my best mate Gary was most definitely her favourite pupil – not that he ever wished for it. He was by far the most troublesome student and, yet, she never dared to discipline him in the same manner she did me.

In truth she probably feared Gary and so chose to prey on the vulnerable instead. Her torment became so much that I dreaded getting up in the morning and trudging my way to school with that sick hollow feeling in my stomach.

I am sure everyone recollects their first time on the hop from school. More than likely it was in your teens, but for me I was just ten and it was pure fear that drove me to it.

I remember that day was one of the longest days of my early life, and for a couple of reasons. Six hours is a long time to fill when you are a child and on your own – especially as you have to remain incognito. I spent half my day hiding in laneways and the rest in the local park. I even remember, while skulking up a lane, my mother unknowingly passed me by on her way to work. Like always her footsteps, or should I say her running, was so familiar to me that I instinctively knew it was her before I saw her. It was customary for my mom to leave everything to the last minute and getting ready for work was one of them.

While hiding, what seemed like a lifetime, in that lane I eventually decided I would be bored and so plucked up the courage to go to school. But as soon as I entered the building and put my hand on the classroom door I resolved that boredom was a better option. With my ear to the door and listening to the voice of the she-devil, my tummy began to weaken and I bolted back out of the school without anyone noticing me. I could not believe my luck. Unfortunately, however, that luck did not last and by the time 3 O'Clock finally came around, and it was time for me to plod my way home, an unexpected surprise awaited me.

While stupidly walking across the green in front of my house, oblivious to the fact that it was not my usual route home from school, who should I meet coming in the opposite direction, but my best mate Gary? As my luck would have it, however, before I could even reach him, out of the corner of my eye I also spotted my mother, who was purposefully marching towards us with a fierce look on her face.

She did not even look at me before she cleverly asked Gary the all-important question.

"Was Robert in school today, Gary?"

To my horror he looked at her as I looked at him, eyes pleading, and answered straight up. "No."

What stunned me even more was the wide smirk on his face as he finally met my desperate stare. I honestly don't think he knew what lay in store for me because if he did he certainly would have not betrayed me in such a callous fashion.

It was some time later that my mother accidently found out the reason I went on the hop that day. While casually talking to a neighbour one night he revealed how his son informed him of the terrible things the teacher inflicted on me throughout the day in class. After that, the story of my mother confronting the she-devil became legend.

*

Though I never forgave Gary for ratting me out that day, he was my best friend while in our youth and we were practically inseparable. For those few years it was a friendship of mutual trust and respect, but most of all it was exciting and meddlesome. There are no words to sum up the character Gary was. He was everything rolled into one. Gary was the type of guy that could have literally been anything he wanted to be. Nothing was too challenging for him, in fact, the more challenging something was the more he revelled in it. I firmly believe he set out every day to find his challenge and would have found life and everything in it quite boring if he had not done so. He was also extremely bright and, though not top of the class, I reckon he could have been if he set his mind to it – it was not cool by anyone's standards though.

He excelled in sport and would always have to be the best at whatever one he chose. The only two games I could match him in were soccer and hurling.

In my young years I had no stronger a passion than in the game of hurling and Gary shared this with me almost to the same level. It was the one game that no matter what his dare I could match him point for point. But where he excelled and others could not even come close were the games he created himself – ones the other boys would not even dare to attempt. At the age of ten, for instance, he challenged me and his other pals to perform cartwheels on a wall that was at least twelve foot in height. We all watched in horrified silence as he effortlessly and fearlessly abandoned his safety to show off his dangerous and crazy stunts.

As he grew older some of those stunts became unbearable to watch as they became a lot more dangerous. That stunt, for instance, progressed from a twelve foot wall to high-rise scaffolding on a derelict building site. That same site was the place where we got up to endless hours of mischief. My younger years of playing with the bow and arrow paid off as Gary and I took aim at the windows in those empty houses. We reckoned the council had an endless amount of glass, as every time we smashed a window it would be miraculously replaced within a few days.

We also accumulated any amount of discarded tools, wood and nails to make our tree house that was to be situated practically dead centre of the park, which is now known as Tymon Park. This was no ordinary tree house as we found the biggest tree in the whole park, which today would be overlooking the lakes. My sister and her friend, Jenny, were included in the building – something which did break the cardinal rule of tree house construction – but, in fairness, they were no ordinary girls.

The house was no ordinary house, either – but a mansion and we believed we gave the council a run for its money when it came to building. The only element it lacked was a window or two but, then again, we reasoned, the council houses that were being built didn't have any either... no thanks to us.

At least we had a stairs carpet, and even a sofa. It was Gary who came up with the ingenious idea of making a hoist, wrapped around a large branch, that pulled the latter up into the tree.

It was around this time, too, that I managed to get a glimpse of a naked woman. Well a lot of naked ladies to be honest. To be even more honest I cannot boast and say that I actually saw them in the flesh, but while playing in one of the many tunnels in the park one of us, and I don't remember who, happened to come upon a stash of hidden treasure. This treasure took the shape of a few dozen magazines that had been thoughtlessly discarded by some dirty old man, no doubt, and were suddenly in the proud possession of two extremely inquisitive young lads.

To say it was an eye-opener would be an understatement and anything else would be downright crude.

*

Christmas is probably most children's favourite time of year. It was not mine, however – Halloween was.

I remember I was still in primary school when my gang of pals and I decided we would have our own Halloween bonfire. The gang consisted of about ten guys, all from the same class, who started in earnest to collect for our bonfire around early September.

Looking back, it's astonishing to realise how disciplined and well-organised we became. My mother would often comment that if I was only half as disciplined when organising my homework I would be a genius.

It became ritualistic, in that every day we would meet at precisely the same time and the same place. Even Sunday, the Sabbath, was considered a day of gathering for us heathens. We had certain rules and guidelines that each one of us had to follow and if broken by any one of us, regardless of rank, we would be banished from the gang. To observe us we were like a miniature band of military soldiers, such was our mission. By year three our scouting had become so good and our mission so popular that even the adults chipped in to give us a helping hand. Without a shadow of a doubt, that third year, we created the biggest bonfire I would ever witness. While scouting in the park one day, Gary and I hit the jackpot. We could not believe our eyes when we stumbled upon a truckload of tyres. We concluded that some garage owner had dumped them and our gratitude was immense – mind you there was a bit of swearing as we were forced to carry them over the muddy and stinking river.

The work was back-breaking but enormously rewarding and by the time Gary and I were finished we had pulled almost fifty tyres out of the river. As my parents' house was the only one with a side entrance, it was decided that the tyres would be stored in my back garden because, unlike most of our other stuff, they were too precious a cargo to hide in ditches. We started to call house to house, and it was surprising the amount of junk people had to give us. The odd smart ass would give us something small for the bonfire and then in return offload his rubbish that clearly wasn't suitable for a bonfire. People had the nerve to give us old washing machines and even a fridge or two. We soon copped on though, and so did the people who gave us such stuff. We would just take the stuff that would burn, and a day or two later we would dump their unwanted junk back in their back garden. We also obtained an endless amount of pallets from a local warehouse, a move I don't think was entirely legal come to think of it now. The pallets were stored in my mate Raymond's, while the discarded sofas were stored in Mark's and the rest was carefully hidden all around the park. When October came around, so huge was our collection, that on the morning of the 31st we all arose at the crack of dawn in order to build our mammoth fire.

And mammoth it was. We had to acquire a telegraph pole to be the centre mast and build everything else against it. By late evening, when we had finally built our elaborate construction, it was a picture of almost anything that could burn; and you could not see the telegraph pole but for a small brown teddy sitting on top of it.

Each and every one of us were extremely proud of our final accomplishment and I remember, as we struck our matches and the first flames took hold, a feeling of great euphoria, and then deep sadness, washed over me.

Looking over at Gary I instinctively knew this would be the last year I would ever collect wood or splash in a murky river with my best mate, who was more like a brother, again.

But although I had that feeling, not even I could have seen the sad and tragic life that lay in store for him.

*

Gary, before his time, outgrew the childish antics of young boys just wanting to have harmless fun. I have a lot of recollections of him, some good, some

16

not so good, but most arise from his ferocious temper. At a young age he had a fierce and dangerous one, that when pronounced, was frightening to behold. He would challenge anyone, regardless of age or size, and if this was not enough he had a do or die attitude in that he would never give up – even when beaten.

I heard many a story through the grapevine of the crazy things Gary got up to with his new-found friends in the following years. Some of the things I believed, some of them I didn't want to believe but imagined to be true. He went down a fast and dangerous road of self-destruction and before long managed to get into all sorts of trouble, the law being just one. Years later while he was serving a stretch in prison I finally plucked up the courage to write to him. My frustration and anger with him was quite evident and among the many questions I was seeking answers to I wanted to know why he mindlessly threw his life away. His reply I will never forget.

He said he was extremely sorry for the pain and anguish he caused everyone, especially his parents, but he never regretted the life he led as it was in his nature to seek the excitement and exhilaration that only driving a stolen car or doing something off the wall, could bring. In some regards that was Gary in a nutshell. He feared nothing and he had to live life on the edge to get his fix. His reckless lifestyle, however, finally caught up with him, as shortly after his prison release he accidently overdosed on heroin and died.

On hearing of his death, it rocked me to the very core. I had so many mixed emotions. I was terribly upset but also profoundly angry. I did not attend Gary's funeral for this very reason and for a long time later I regretted it.

*

A person has only to step inside a Christian church to be reminded of the suffering of the Virgin Mary while her son was dying on the cross. Her pain is quite evident in the countless pictures and statues that depict the crucifixion of the Lord and if ever a woman suffered similar pain it was Gary's mother.

Not only did she have to bear the pain of his tragic death, but just a few years later her only other son, Simon, died the very same way. You could say it was practically identical as his death was also shortly after his release from prison too.

It is almost inconceivable the suffering of these parents and I am not going to try to put it into words. Gary and his brother left it all in their wake because of their misguided lives and futile deaths.

What broke my heart even more was that after Simon's death their father got Cancer, a battle he lost. It was obviously too much for any woman to bear because soon after Gary and Simon's mother succumbed to the vicious disease and died within a year of her beloved husband.

I was extremely fortunate in that I did not go down the same road as Gary and I put this down to the fact that my mother sent me to my grandparents' farm throughout the summer months, to keep me out of mischief.

I have to say that I will be eternally grateful to her for doing that because despite the fact that my fate would eventually take me down my own harrowing road, it was certainly a hell of a lot better than the one Gary took.

Chapter Six

IN the weeks and months that followed my accident my sister Loreena became like a mother hen, without the patronising, whereas my younger sister Natasha became outwardly rebellious towards everyone – especially me. On no occasion whatsoever would she consider doing anything for me.

I recall one day in particular when her then boyfriend and I were sitting in the sitting room listening to television. Natasha was in the kitchen, I assumed making dinner. From there she eventually called to her boyfriend, declaring that the dinner was on the table. Assuming that she had made one for me too I strolled in to find nothing prepared for me.

"Where is mine?" I asked.

"In the fridge," came the answer.

"You mean in the oven."

"No, in the fridge. If you want dinner you can make it yourself. You'd think you were helpless, but you're not. You're too fucking lazy, that's all that's wrong with you," she hissed.

"You're nothing but a selfish bitch," I bellowed, surprising myself. "And what's wrong with that damn boyfriend of yours?"

There were other occasions similar to this and I couldn't fathom what I had done for her to treat me in such a manner. *How had she come to dislike me so much?*

It was only some time later that I came to realise and understand why she reacted in the way she did. It was by no means intentional, but because of her youth she felt excluded, like she was left in the dark when it came to any discussion to do with me, or what possibly lay in store for me – if anything. The truth of the matter was that we were all in the dark during those early months and although every one of us was teetering on a knife's edge Natasha was just more vocal in expressing it.

She was annoyed that everyone was making such a fuss over me and, as she saw it, doing practically everything for me. This, of course, was true and, admittedly, I even gloated over the fact that I was being pampered; but Natasha had more foresight than any of us gave her credit for and knew quite well that I was more than capable of doing things for myself.

In part, the problem was that she just wanted her old brother back.

*

19

During those early months everything I attempted to do was exhausting. This was not just due to the fact that I was recovering from three major surgeries, but I literally had to retrain my brain to do the simplest of tasks. Nothing came automatically anymore and ordinary everyday functions were proving quite difficult. The little things I always took for granted were now cumbersome and tiring. There was a stage when I even wondered if I was slightly brain damaged from the accident, due to the fact that my concentration and movement had become extremely sluggish. Not only had my reflexes dramatically slowed but performing anything that involved any dexterity demanded tremendous concentration and effort.

Although my reflexes were slow I deliberately moved slower too, so as not to make clumsy mistakes. At the dinner table for instance, I would slowly reach for something, like a cup or glass, so as not to knock it over. Other times I would forget where I placed whatever the hell utensil I was using. It was for this very reason my mother tended to do everything for me, from putting butter on my bread to sugar in my tea, before stirring my cup. I had become helplessly indulgent and lazy, practically overnight – and I knew it.

I would not remove myself from the bed until late afternoon and only then it was to lounge lazily in the armchair for the rest of the day. It was because of all this that it was somewhat daunting the first day I ventured outside to take a short stroll around the block with my two sisters. Even that was a task, as remarkably my coordination and balance – just for bloody walking – was mysteriously unhinged, and I was like a child learning to take my first steps. To everyone else I looked like a drunken, six foot tall, grown man falling over his feet.

Frustration slowly gave way to anger, returning to increased frustration and self-loathing. I secretly berated myself for the slightest clumsy mistake, to the extent that I eventually ended up doing nothing. Friends faithfully called to remind me of their existence and a life previously led. I laughed when they laughed, as they desperately tried to include me in their world – one which I no longer felt a part of – and I could feel myself simply slipping away.

It was a talent I never realised I had, but I fooled everyone by outwardly appearing calm and totally in control. Close friends even commented on how reasonable I was with my plummeted misfortune; declaring that, for them, keeping it together and not cracking up would have been impossible.

I kept sane in those first few months, simply by focussing all my thoughts and energy away from reality and into a fantasy world where I lived and breathed a girl I assumed I was in love with. From early morning to last thing at night she lived in my mind to a point where I could not, or would not, focus on anything else. She had become the perfect distraction and, yes, my thoughts and fantasies where clean (well most of them, with the odd exception!) but I will never forget the day the world I had created came crumbling down with such force that I was thrown from my denial back to reality, with a thump.

I had finally plucked up the courage, after months of torturous secrecy, to approach her with my truth. We were in a local hotel after a Joe Dolan concert, having a few drinks, and I remember sitting next to her like an awkward, lovesick puppy.

It wasn't long, however, before I found out that her powers of perception were a lot more in tune than mine. She could detect my clumsy shyness straight away.

"You're very quiet tonight," she exclaimed.

"No I am not," I said defensively.

"What's wrong?"

"Nothing."

"You have been staring into space all night."

"Is that meant to be funny?" I snapped.

"You know I didn't mean it like that you smart bastard."

"I know, sorry."

"Shall I make this easy for you?

"What do you mean?"

"For fuck's sake, I know you fancy me." She was not one to mince her words.

I was struck dumb and went from pale to red and back to pale.

"Well, do you or do you not? she demanded.

"What, fancy you?"

"I would want to be a right gobshite not to have noticed. I was just wondering when you would pluck up the courage to say it to me."

"Well, do you fancy me?" I asked, blunt but hopeful.

"No," she replied.

It was like blunt force trauma to the heart. I was crushed, embarrassed, devastated. I didn't know where to turn.

"Thanks a lot," was all I could manage.

Then, taking me by the hand her voice became very serious.

"Robert, I love you very much, but not in the way you want me to."

"Oh and what way is that?" My sarcastic defence mechanism only served to make me more unattractive to her I am sure, but I had nothing else.

"Don't be stupid, you bloody know what way, but I can't…"

"You'll probably tell me I am like a brother to you next," I declared.

"Fuck off," was her reply. "Anyway you don't really love me."

"That's crap," I said.

"Do you not think I know what is really going on in that head and heart of yours?" she asked.

"Oh, you can read minds now, can you?"

"Listen to me you smart shit..."

And as I listened to her it was as though she could really look inside my mind and even my very soul. She told me exactly what was really going on inside of me. That I did not really love her but was using my mixed emotions on her as a substitute, in an effort to block out the depths of my despair.

"How did you come up with that crock of shit?" I asked in confused anger. "Fuck you then," she said as she stood up out of her chair and walked away.

A few minutes later she reluctantly came back to me, to take me home. I didn't want to go with her, but I had no choice.

To make things worse she noticed my pain and humiliation, and wrapped her arms around me before giving me a kiss she would her brother.

I now know that this was a considerable amount of insight and tremendous consideration for a young lady of just seventeen, but back then it was just a crushing blow to my heart.

As we drove home Michael Bolton was singing some poxy song with the lyrics, *when all that I've been living for is gone* and I could not get out of the car quick enough. At that moment and time all I wanted to do was scream. I could take no more agony and this was the catalyst that made me finally snap.

As I closed the door to my room a frightening mix of emotions came tearing out, uncontrollably, and on impulse I began to repeatedly pound my fists against my bedroom wall – to the point where I collapsed with spent energy and exhaustion. While pounding the hell out of the wall my family, in its wisdom, did not intervene and it was only when I lay in a painful state on the floor that my sis came into the room and, without saying a word, embraced me and pointed at the wall. Through the pain I managed a frown as she brought me over to the damage I had created on the plasterboard. She then placed my hand along the huge ridge, gaping hole and crack from one end of the wall to the other – all left behind by my furious fists. I involuntarily shuddered with the realisation of what I had done.

A few days later my parents arrived home and presented me with a punchbag, which was strategically hung from the rafters in my room.

My mother, Margaret, me and my sisters, Loreena and Natasha

Loreena and I (top right and above)

ROB'S BLIND AMBITION

By BARRY O'KELLY

■ DUBLINER Robbie Dowdall is set to scale new heights — by being the first blind Irishmen to climb Kilimanjaro.

He will be lead by fellow Dub, Tony Maguire from Cabra, as part of an 80-strong team who will start to tackle the 20,000 ft African mountain on September 9th.

24-year-old Robbie was blinded in a car accident four years ago.

"We're all very excited about it — particularly Robbie," climbing fanatic, Tony told The Star.

■ The team has been planning the expedition for a year and a half.

But Robbie has only been preparing for the last six months.

"They reckon only one in five of the team will make it to the top — but we expect Robbie to be among the people who make it," said Tony.

Adventure-mad Robbie has already walked the Brazillian Rain Forests.

■ "He's also cycled from Sydney to Brisbane — that's 700 miles. He has skied in St Johann in Austria, and is a keen absailer," said Tony, from Faussagh Road.

"I don't know if it was just his eyes that were affected in the accident," he joked.

The trip to Kilamanjiro is intended to raise money for the Richmond Brain Researach Foundation and the National Council for the Blind.

Taking on Kilimanjaro

Kilimanjaro

My sherpa and me having climbed Kilimanjaro

Myself and the Kilimanjaro climb team

Capturing an Elephant on safari in Kenya

Terrifying Crocodiles - I had an unfortunate incident with one!

A local Eagle handler

Maasai warriors dancing

Myself and Tom with an enormous Turtle!

Trekking down the Amazon

Brazil

Getting to grips with a baby Croc

Snake charmers – The Snake that dumped on Mike!

Iguazu Falls

Iguazu region

Fancy dress in Brazil

Myself, Mick and the gang in Brazil

Myself and Theo cycling in the US for NCBI

Myself and my first Guide Dog, Libby

Chapter Seven

OVER the weeks that followed I did what we Irish do best – buried my feelings. In general I talked crap in the pub while my mother continued talking to God.

During this time she brought me to every faith healing freak around. It was my belief, however, that if I was not going to be healed by the almighty himself then no nutter proclaiming divine intervention and laying their hands on me, had a chance.

Now it probably sounds as though I had a personal chip on my shoulder with God, and I somehow blamed him for the accident and consequently losing my sight, but that's not the case – exactly...

While I did not blame him for causing the accident I did accuse him of not stopping it or evening helping the surgeon in the numerous operations that followed. It's human nature, I think, that when tragedy strikes us poor old God naturally gets the blame and we lash out at him. It is the easy solution and an alternative to looking inside of ourselves for healing.

So naturally I lay all the blame at God's heavenly door.

Why the hell not? I thought, sure he could take the criticism, he being God and all.

People either turn to God or totally walk away when tragedy strikes. In our hour of need we turn to him for favour, but when not granted we walk away. I suppose I was somewhere in the middle. I honestly did not care where I stood with him. I did not care because I was totally numb at the time.

My grandad's outlook on the situation was amusing.

His power of healing was as good as any of the freak healers we went seeking the assistance of, and coming from a farming background he had many old remedies that were often put to use in various situations. When a sheep formed a cataract over the eye it was known that my grandad would chew a great chunk of tobacco and then spit this into the poor unfortunate animal's socket. Informing people of this he claimed it miraculously worked by burning the cataract away. Surely, in the great man's infinite wisdom, he knew in his heart the situation was a lot worse than this, but I reckon this was his way of giving hope when he knew there was little.

When it came to strength my mother had plenty of her own, but whatever reserves she needed she found them in my grandad; because even though a silent witness he was the tower of strength that would be there if called upon.

And just as my mother relied on my grandfather's shoulder, I was hoping the rocks I could lean on where his four sons – my uncles. Throughout my teenage years my uncles, my mother's brothers, played a huge role in, and had a huge influence on, my life. When in their company I almost felt as though I was the fifth brother. From my early teenage years, at every chance I got – this being nearly every weekend and most certainly my summer holidays – I would spend my time joyously working on my grandad's farm with the four of them.

After spending my childhood in Kilbeggan, I never totally adapted to the lifestyle that living in Tallaght presented. Although my grandad's farm was only about five miles from the centre of Tallaght, in the beautiful valley of Glenasmole in the Dublin hills, it was, for me, a world away and here I spent the most wonderful times of my teenage years.

Unless you have spent some time on a farm or have been reared on one, you could not possibly conceive of or understand the wonderful, multifaceted ways of rural life in comparison to those of the city. When there, I felt extremely privileged to awaken every morning to the varying sounds of the farm – the noisy and cantankerous cockerel, the geese with their contemptuous outbursts if someone or something passed within close proximity of them, the purr of the tractor and so much more. Whether it was animal noise or heavy farm machinery that awoke me, my granny would always have a breakfast so big and nourishing that it would last a little runt like me until midnight.

My granny was a caring and loving woman who idolised my grandfather and spent most of her life toiling over the kitchen sink and stove, preparing endless meals for her adored family. Everything she had she gave to them, but there was one vice she held dear and I was the only other person who knew about it. This was her secret smoking habit.

One day while she was taking a stroll across the back lane I came upon her with a smoke in her hand. I don't know who got the bigger shock but both of us jumped simultaneously. At ten I wasn't sure what to say but I was innocent and only too delighted to be sworn to secrecy. Years later I would realise that practically everyone knew and, in fact, enjoyed making her squirm over it. I remember one day when my granny was coming out of the hen house puffing away, unaware that her eldest son was watching her. My uncle didn't say a thing but approached her and when she noticed him she forced the cigarette into her apron pocket. He kept her talking for over five minutes and it was with considerable discomfort that she attempted to hide the smoke rising from the pocket.

It was clear to me that my uncle was getting great pleasure out of my gran's misfortune and when she eventually made her escape he turned and looked at me with a big grin, before jokingly telling me to fetch a bucket of water and put my granny out.

*

Another great story from the farm was the day my grandfather went to the hill to gather sheep without his teeth. For a man in his seventies he was a tower of strength and could function and complete any task on the farm with the energy and dexterity of a man half his age. On this particular day he and his loyal dog, Shep, headed off up the hill to gather sheep and send them on to higher pastures. The dog was an old hand at this task and everything should have been going smoothly but soon after my grandad could be heard cursing and swearing as, flushed and hot-tempered, he descended the mountain with Shep in hasty retreat.

When he got home and caught his breath no one dared laugh as he described getting to the top of the hill and putting his fingers in his mouth to whistle to Shep – but nothing came out. It then dawned on him that he had forgotten to put his false teeth in that morning. It wasn't that which annoyed him most, however, it was the fact that the old dog looked at him in bewilderment waiting for his commands without doing a thing.

Without the whistle commands the dog just stood there looking perplexed at the sheep and my grandad, who was furious with him because as he reckoned the dog should have automatically known what to do, as he had "done it often enough." After a half an hour of ranting and everyone sitting tight and listening it was my brave granny who eventually ventured, "I don't know how that poor old dog puts up with you. Sure it was not the dog that forgot his teeth."

With that everyone burst out laughing, the tension draining from the room… until they looked again at the big man, whose expression stopped them in their tracks.

*

It was about six months after my accident that my friend and I took a ramble up through the reservoir, which is situated close to my grandfather's farm, and coincidentally we happened to come upon one of the fields where my uncles were bailing hay. Without hesitation my friend, Mick, and I decided to pitch in and lend a hand. In my naivety I took to the task assuming it would be like old times – unfortunately I was wrong. What happened after was heart-wrenchingly revealing of the physche of my extended family.

Within seconds of getting involved the atmosphere changed from one of gaiety to anxious tension. These big burly men, the heroes of my childhood,

25

gave in to a palpable awkwardness, reducing them to practical silence.

There was nothing for it – they could not be drawn out, hard and all as we tried, and the result was that I did not stay long in the field that day. As I left I fought to hold back my anger, frustration and tears because I didn't blame them – I could just, ironically, see clearly for the first time, that the accident had not just robbed me of my sight but also my old life.

I knew instinctively, leaving the field with my broken heart that day, that I was leaving the old Robert back there forever and it is that guy that still lives in my uncle's memories, I presume, today.

Chapter Eight

THAT day had a profound effect on my life and I came to the realisation that I could no longer live in the past. I was stuck with my predicament and I had to start tackling the present situation.

It was because of this that I decided I was no longer prepared to travel back and forth to the hospital without getting definite answers and in the April, eight months after my first surgery, I confronted my surgeons, head on.

Subconsciously, I can see now, I had resigned myself to the fact that there was no hope of me ever regaining my sight and so I wasn't overly shocked when it was said directly to me. It turned out that my right eye was so extremely damaged that there was no possibility of any response from it, and although they had been hoping that with time there would be some improvement in my left eye, it wasn't happening.

At this time it was, again, my mother who was the tower of strength for me and although she took an involuntary gasp (I think if she had not been sitting she would have collapsed) at his words she found the strength to carry on for me. Even in her paralysing shock she was not willing to give up on her son and requested another opinion. My surgeon did not hesitate in recommending a renowned surgeon of the same calibre, across the water in Manchester city.

Two weeks later, while my parents and I were sitting in the surgery of the eminent eye surgeon in Britain, he announced the prognosis that finally drove the nail home.

"Robert, I'll give it to you straight. I'm sure you will appreciate that."

"Please do," I nodded, not particularly nervous but wanting, at the same time, for it to be over with.

"If you are ever to have a chance of seeing again it's a simple as this – you will need a brain transplant."

This time it was my turn to gasp... *a brain transplant?!*

"I don't understand..."

"The optic nerve is so badly damaged it's beyond repair Robert. You're only hope would be to have a transplant and really, realistically, that's not an option at all."

So there I had it.

In all sincerity the end result did not surprise me one bit and the trip was, admittedly, just an effort to allay my parents doubts. I had total faith in my own surgeon, but it wasn't just about me.

Did I contemplate suicide?

Of course I did.

Not two weeks before, after my surgeon gave it to us straight, on a crazy impulse I decided to take a walk to the local park without anyone's knowledge. It was a miracle that I did not walk out under a bus or get hit by a car while crossing the road to enter the park, because all I could see was a bare shadow.

I was full of despair, foreboding and anger. *Did I want to be here?* No was the only answer I had at that time. The accident, the months that followed, the hope and the crushing despair were swirling around in my mind. *What was the point? Why would I want to live this life?* I had no hope, no prospects…I didn't want to fight.

There was no specific plan for suicide. I guess I hoped that the elements would take over – traffic, bad roads, water…anything. I didn't care how it happened, I just wanted it to be over.

While fumbling my way through the park, however, I was unaware that Jackie, the faithful family dog, was accompanying my every faltering step. I only became aware of this when the park attendant shouted over to me that my dog should be on a lead. At first, in my ignorance, I didn't realise he was even talking to me.

But he wasn't giving up and I soon realised it was my arch enemy – the same ranger who patrolled the park every day when I, on my way to secondary school, would take the shortcut regardless of his numerous warnings.

Like my mother, who was always late for events, I was always deliberately late for school and would come tearing through the park with little regard for the nesting ducks and swans. My argument with Mr Scarecrow, on the occasions that he would catch me, was that he created more of a disturbance among his beloved birds than I ever could, with his bellowing and shouting. If he just left me alone I would fly by without ruffling a feather. I even went so far as to explain to him (and I still don't know how he didn't clobber me) that the only feathers that seemed to be ruffled by me were his.

I would like to say that he saved me from doing something drastic or that he rescued me on the day he escorted me, and my precious dog, out of the park – but he did not. The only thing that stopped me from ending my life that day was the fact that I could not put my parents through any more torture and the inevitable life sentence my death would bestow on them.

When you are at rock bottom and the devil is climbing on your back, you can choose one of two things. You can let him drag you under, or kick him in the balls, pick yourself up, struggle forward and start living again.

I had enough of hell and as there were no more 'what ifs' to dwell upon, it was time for me to get on with my life and make the best of what I had.

Now that I knew my circumstances were permanent, there was fuck all anyone else could do, and I was dammed if I was going to spend any more time feeling sorry for myself, and crying about the past. If anything, my attitude changed almost overnight and where once I was the perfect example of a delicate shell, that if touched would crumble, I suddenly put up an exterior shell so hard that no one could penetrate.

My blindness was, by then, something I saw as an enemy that invaded my existence and needed to be challenged and conquered at every turn. I was not going to be seen as a blind person, but a person who is blind.

So I was ready to face whatever challenges lay in store for me, but even my false bravado and steely stubbornness could not have prepared me for some of the life changing challenges I was yet to be faced with.

Chapter Nine

IN order for me to confront my challenges and to acquire the skills I would need to get on with my life, I was automatically registered with the organisation known as the National Council for the Blind. Its function, among some others, is to provide services for the blind and visually impaired.

Some of the training is in providing skills to individuals so they can gain sufficient independence in whichever environment they find themselves in. This can be simply in the kitchen, managing the everyday task of cooking or learning about adapted technology that will provide the tools and knowledge that a person may need to function in a working environment.

The first social worker that was assigned to me was ever so efficient, and after a lot of formalities and signing of documents, it was official – I was registered blind with the state. From there on in I was entitled to whatever the Republic of Ireland graciously bestowed upon me.

The first visit to the centre is still very vivid in my mind. It was quite daunting but only because of the image of it that I had built in my imagination. I presumed the place would be totally removed from the real world where able-bodied people functioned and lived.

My first encounter with another blind person was when I was introduced to the lady who was going to have the surmountable task of trying to encourage me to learn Braille. Regardless of how determined I was to learn certain skills to improve my quality of life, learning Braille was not one of them; and no matter how hard my poor unfortunate teacher insisted that it was a necessity for me, her comments just went in one ear and out the other.

It was not long before she realised that no matter how hard she tried to teach me, it was never going to happen. It was not that I found learning Braille tough – on the contrary, I picked it up quite easily as I soon figured out the formation of the dots and the words they formed – the problem was that I never bothered studying or practicing my little knowledge and subsequently never gained sufficient speed to read anything with exact accuracy or at an acceptable rate.

So I gave up on Braille, because with no patience or inclination to spend half an hour reading a page (that by the time I had reached the end of I had totally forgotten) it was a lost cause.

*

The effect of losing one's sight, emotionally, is almost indescribable, but it is the repercussions of this that are even more debilitating.

Independence, or lack of it, was the first casualty that plagued me in my early days of rehabilitation. Being totally dependent on someone else for practically every move you make, to put it bluntly, is an absolute bitch.

There are many things one loses when the sense of sight is gone and I'm sure if you ask other visually impaired people you will more than likely get numerous answers as to what disturbed them the most, but for me I can say, without hesitation, it was losing that independence.

I remember, as a teenager, being in Dublin city centre one day and I watched with fascination as a blind man, seemingly with little or no effort, negotiated his way around varying obstacles with the aid of a white stick. My mother, who was with me at the time, remarked that it was ignorant of me to stare, and then followed this with a clip behind the ear. I then casually asked why it mattered if I stared as the blind man could not see me staring.

As a teenager I could not get my freedom quick enough and this did not change in me despite the huge obstacle of blindness. I just had to metaphorically step into that blind man's shoes if I was ever to gain the independence I desired.

*

The overwhelming responsibility of teaching me mobility with a white stick lay in the hands of a mobility officer who was, yet again, provided to me by the National Council. In my ignorance I assumed I would be tearing around town in no time whatsoever – or least down my own road and around the local area. This certainly was not to be, as before I could learn, or even contemplate getting to a desired destination, I was informed that technique, with regard to walking with a stick, was paramount.

I figured that all I had to do was swing the stick in all directions and keep walking until my it whacked off something, then walk around it. And what could be so hard about that?

I realised my ignorance pretty quickly, however, as I was guided through the varying techniques of handling my cane – none of which involved recklessly swinging it. Rather, in an almost graceful motion, the stick was to be moved in the shape of an arc not more than two feet in front of me. The left leg, needed to be was dominantly in front the stick, while the stick came from the right.

Now to anyone else this may seem ridiculously easy, but coordination is harder than it looks, excuse the pun. Without sounding too boastful though, I soon picked up this style with a fashion that was entirely unique to me and as such I was ready to take my new skill out into the world.

I had been tirelessly practicing and developing my technique inside of a big hall in the local secondary school and although safety was paramount, quite frankly I was getting bored of the constant repetition. I say this without malice or blame towards my instructor, but I needed something more intense and challenging and the once a fortnight visit from her was just not good enough for me and my plans to move forward. I'm not sure if the resources where overwhelmed, underfunded or simply not there, but sitting week in and week out twiddling my thumbs and waiting for things to happen was not part of my agenda, so my mother began to make inquiries about receiving training elsewhere.

It was my surgeon who eventually came up with the solution that would finally catapult me forward and onto the right path. What my doctor suggested would take me to Torquay in Britain where I would undergo intensive training in various modules, specifically guiding me towards independence and the capacity to do everyday chores that most able-bodied people take for granted.

I remember being extremely nervous and secretly wishing I didn't have to go, but it was a necessary evil that I had to face if I ever wanted to make any meaningful progress.

For me, Britain may as well have been a million miles away and if the plane journey was not bad enough the several hours on the train were even worse. Both my parents travelled with me and there was an awkward silence the entire time as they attuned to my tension and feeling of foreboding. Let's face it, I was leaving the seclusion of my home and going to a country that, at the time, was not on the friendliest of terms with its neighbours.

So like most Irish, and with me being a true patriot, I carried an element of animosity and backward thinking over with me.

Saying goodbye to my parents I put on a brave face as I was sure they were doing the very same. I may have only hugged my father once or twice in my life previous to this time, but that departure was one occasion we didn't think twice about it. If ever there were parents made of true grit it's mine.

I think it was harder for them to leave me there, but they knew in their hearts it was the only option for their son, if he was ever to regain any sort of normality, self-respect, pride and much more.

I truly believe when they said their farewell they left every ounce of their soul, love and compassion with me in the hope that I would come back to them, regardless of what I learned.

All they wanted was a son with hope and expectations in his heart – essentially the one they had lost that fateful night on September 11th, 1989.

Chapter Ten

I DON'T think I had ever felt so alone as the first few days after my parents went home. Many jumbled thoughts ran though my mind, but the one constant was my saviour – I was resolute that whatever lay ahead of me I would face it with all of my ability and determination.

I wanted to go home a different person and hoped, in doing so, I would not just give hope to myself, but also my parents.

Though never seeing the training centre or its surrounding grounds, my mind's eye still has a vivid image of many of its little details. Of course this image is different to a visual image but nevertheless it is probably even more detailed in other ways, as it was here that I learned to awaken my other senses – ones which so many sighted people take for granted.

Before embarking on my various modules I was assigned a mobility officer so I could get familiar with my new surrounds. This alone was exhausting enough and I had not even started my other classes. My new mobility officer was a former paratrooper and at first I found him much too militant and serious. Those of you, who have ever had the great pleasure of watching the magnificent Star Wars trilogies, will recall in one of the movies where the hero, Luke Skywalker, embarks on his mystical training to become a Jedi Knight. As part of this he is trained to heighten his senses to enable him to become aware of everything while in the dark – my training was similar. Unlike him, however, I had a white stick instead of a light sabre, but it did equally as well in challenging any adversary. Disappointingly though mine were not as strange or as colourful as the ones the famous Jedi came up against. I had to make do with the odd parked car, lamppost and litterbin. Sometimes when encountering one or two of these obstacles I did wish my white stick was actually a light sabre so I could magically vaporise the damn object into oblivion.

With constant repetition, however, I began to get familiar with my alien world and as I began to identify and recognise my obstacles, my frustration lessened and they no longer became objects to strike out at, but ones to simply identify and casually walk around.

My instructor, with his military training and background, was a huge influence. Before ever taking a single step he would take me into an almost trance-like state, with shallow breathing, to calm the nerves. Then, in a very serious tone he would say; "Now, young Robert, remember mistakes are only made when one is nervous."

He would then continue to expertly explain how I should use my environment, with its varying sounds, as a guide. Rather than seeing obstacles as an obstruction, he said to use them as a destination and landmark.

He taught me so many things, like using wind direction and the strength of it to determine weather in open ground and even to use its vibration. So exciting, his class became, that I no longer walked nervously like a stiff old man waiting to fall over but the young chap that I was, with reassurance and confidence. Like the martial arts films I had so fondly watched in previous years, where the great master passed his infinite wisdom on to his devoted pupil, I felt like the young warrior at the feet of my own.

After unloading all his knowledge he took me aside one day and in his most serious tone said to me; "Robert, I'm going to give you the most important advice I can give you so please don't forget it."

I waited with baited breath.

"If all your training fails you and you find yourself lost, you have a fucking tongue in your head, so use it."

I almost fell from the chair I was sitting on. He then burst into the one and only laugh I ever heard from him. It was a surreal, but very funny, moment – and I still consider it one of the best pieces of advice I have ever received.

After a few days in the training centre I learned that the majority of students came, like me, to be blind in later life rather than being born that way.

Some had lost it due to various eye diseases, which I had been completely unaware of but came to find out there are many of and starting with every alphabetical letter too. The majority of those who did not lose their sight due to disease lost it tragically in varying accidents.

There were two guys who lost theirs in the same way I did – motor accidents. Another guy lost his when the battery he was charging from a car exploded in his face and the acid sprayed into his eyes. Every person had their own story, but the ones I found most profound and disturbing were the young men who had lost their sight as victims of the violence and hatred in the north of Ireland.

For this very reason I kept a low profile and deliberately avoided these men. Being the only Irish guy I was fearful I might become a victim of what I assumed would be a repulsion of anything Irish. I assumed they would be carrying huge chips on their shoulders and that I would be the target of their bitterness and derision because, let's be honest here, if the shoe was on the other foot I think I would need to vent my frustration.

I couldn't have been more wrong.

One evening the two of them came knocking on the door of my room

34

with a request that I go for a drink with them. I was cautious at first but in the end agreed and as drinks flowed and tongues loosened, they openly told me of their tour of duty in Belfast and adjoining counties of Northern Ireland. They recounted their different events and the build-up to how each, individually, lost their sight – one by landmine and shrapnel, the other a vicious beating.

I cringed waiting for one or both of them to point the finger but instead one asked; "So, Robert, how did you lose your sight?"

I have to admit I was half afraid to elaborate, so I simply said "car crash." "What do you mean a car crash? What happened?" he pressed.

So I told them my story and afterwards there was complete silence for a few minutes before the same guy uttered; "What a fucking bummer, that must have been tough."

"Sure it's a lot better than what you guys went through," I replied genuinely.

"No, it's fucking worse mate."

"How could it be worse?" I stammered, surprising myself as I struggled to hold back the tears. "What you went through is atrocious. I can't even begin to imagine… I'm just so sorry…"

"What the hell have you to be sorry about?" he interrupted.

"Well, I'm Irish," is all I could say.

"What's that got to do with anything you daft bugger? Nothing, that's what. We don't hold any bitterness or hatred towards the Irish – especially you! We knew what the risks were in accepting a tour of Northern Ireland and we're at peace with that. As soldiers it is easier to accept your fate when you accept that going into battle."

I hadn't realised I was holding my breath until that second and as I exhaled he added; "As for your sight loss, just being out on an innocent night, now that's a bastard."

We all agreed before the other man uttered his first words in minutes; "Did you even get laid in the end that night?"

"No," I laughed.

"Now that is a fucking tragedy," he replied.

After that night, for the first time, my eyes were opened to the narrow-minded and twisted thoughts I had been carrying for so long. Before I even met these guys I had formed a negative opinion of them and if the truth be known, I was condemning them for ever occupying the north of Ireland. I went as far as thinking they almost deserved their lousy predicament… but then I found myself sitting with them, sharing a drink with them and thanks to their open-armed approach my opinions were changed rapidly. They didn't harbour an ounce of resentment in their hearts. They, like me, were just trying to get on with their lives and looking forward to a more positive future without any regrets of the past.

I came away that night a lot warmer of the heart and lighter of the shoulders having learned so much from these lads, who where too busy trying to get on with their lives to be bothered with poisonous thoughts.

Chapter Eleven

AS the weeks passed I found myself slowly finding my feet in the training centre in Torquay and for the first time since I had lost my sight I felt I belonged to the world again.

I no longer felt like an outcast just taking the odd glimpse at society and the world around me. This place, which was dedicated to the education and rehabilitation of the blind, did not shut itself, or us, off from the rest of society and that was vital for my progression. While there, there was never a time I felt patronised, incompetent or incapable. On the contrary, I was encouraged and told that blindness was not a boundary. That, yes, it was a nuisance and often extremely difficult to cope with, but nevertheless I could and would learn to live a good life with it – and slowly but surely I found it easier to believe that.

Regardless, however, of how I excelled at my new subjects, Braille remained a sore point. Eventually though, I was introduced to the technology that, despite being in its infancy development-wise, would change my life forever. It was a machine that could identify and miraculously read print, with just a few mistakes along the way. My Braille teacher, with twenty-twenty vision, could not see the future for this machine, of course, and doubted it would ever take off – but thankfully she was wrong. Proof of this is my own machine that almost two decades later is incredibly more advanced and I would be lost without it.

There is no doubt that there is no comparison between the technology today and that of two decades ago and, without exaggeration, there is almost something new on the market every week to assist a visually impaired person. And even though it was a Godsend I can see now how technology creates such a fine line between being absolutely necessary in your everyday life and creating a sense of security so huge it renders you lazy. I used this machine to replace Braille but I had to be careful not to rely on it too heavily at the same time.

It was also at the centre in Torquay that I discovered a passion which stays with me today (but is probably the last thing anyone would expect a blind person to do, bar drive!) and that is take up the intricate skill of woodturning. It was the motto of the centre, though, to try everything and if one thing failed then at least you had tried – it took me a long time to realise that it was this motto that made me like it so much there.

Fortunately I took to woodturning like a duck to water, which was ironic because when I had my sight I was hopeless at woodwork and my secondary school master often pointed it out to me. He would inform me that my mind and hands were not working in coordination with each other because my mind was always racing miles ahead – eager to see the end product and not taking the time to delicately take the wood through the step by step process, needed for it to see completion.

However, now that I was totally relying on my hands, my mind had no other option but to slow down. For the first time in my life my hands and mind were working in perfect coordination and, if anything, my hands were seeing things my mind and eyes would previously have willingly skipped over and accepted. My hands simply would not accept anything that was less than perfect.

So enamoured was I with my newfound skill that when I returned home I approached the National Council for the Blind, hoping there would be a chance that they might teach it. But the organisation regarded it as far too dangerous and the insurance too high to ever teach a totally blind person – a liability.

I did not let this unfortunate misconception deter me, though, and ever the stubborn mule I eventually found someone who was more than willing to teach me and who was up for the challenge as much as I was.

It is the likes of these people, who could see past my disability and meet me halfway, that I am eternally grateful to...

Chapter Twelve

THOUGH extremely daunting in the beginning, I can now look back on my time in the training centre in Torquay with the fondest of memories and extreme gratitude. I no longer felt isolated from the rest of the world, and while learning and acquiring numerous skills I was also evolving emotionally, and was slowly regaining my confidence and self worth. As you can imagine when losing one's sight, self-esteem seems to disappear and mine escaped into the dark recesses of my mind – at eighteen there is no worse feeling.

This was most obvious when it came to the torturous lack of that same self-esteem with the opposite sex. Looking back, in fact, this was probably the biggest psychological battle I had to overcome. Yes, the physical challenges are huge to say the least, but that is all they were to me – challenges. If anything I found them a healthy distraction from the suppressed fears and doubts I was really having. I was more than willing to show the world that, ok, I was blind and shit happens, but that with hard work and determination I was equal to the next person... but deep in my heart it is not how I felt.

The awkward nature of blindness and the everyday challenges that come with it are often tangible, and with time I got to grips with those. The psychological baggage that comes with it, however, is a whole different ball game; and no matter how well I was doing to improve my physical circumstances with regards to independence and self sufficiency, it was the irrational emotions that were slowly wearing me down and chipping away at my heart and soul.

There was no bigger a kick to my psyche than at the age of eighteen when I came to the realisation that no female would ever be bothered having a relationship with me. I was convinced I would remain a dreaded virgin for many years to come. Alright, I know it might be hard to believe that there is such a thing as an eighteen-year-old virgin but back then that was not all that unusual. No scratch that statement – it's not true. I was just what you might call, a late starter.

The ironic thing was that I was surrounded constantly with the companionship of the opposite sex, but it was all about feminine support and platonic kindness. It was as though me being blind had blinded these young women to the fact that regardless of me not being able to see, everything else was working quite perfectly and I was itching to put my desires into practice.

To my extreme annoyance and frustration, however, I had to accept my fate as an agony aunt to my numerous female friends, as time and again they came to me seeking advice and pouring their hearts out.

The worst part of it was having to listen to their uncensored and extremely intimate encounters. Now, while you might ask what the hell am I complaining about, you have to understand that, at that time, it was quite abnormal for a young lady to openly detail such intimacy. But they felt they could because they simply saw me as one of the girls and not a threat to their femininity.

"For fuck's sake!" I wanted to roar.

Could they not see that I was one of those guys they so openly talked about? I longed to be desired and lusted over. Instead, however, I was treated like a gay best friend; who at the time it was assumed weren't like other men who only thought with their penises. They thought with their hearts and a rational understanding that straight men were incapable of.

Holy Christ, I figured I was not only not regarded as a typical full-blooded male, but in these girls' eyes I had become an honorary member of the girly club with gay status. This tore at my heart not to mention somewhere else that was slowly driving me bonkers! As you can imagine my thinking back then was totally irrational but I could not help the way I felt for my self-esteem, and any hint of confidence I had, was totally shattered.

I'm not going to boast and state that I was a great one for pulling young women before I lost my sight because when it came to girls I was actually quite shy... well if I fancied one. I would freeze over before I would ever pluck up the courage to reveal how I felt. So when it came to affairs of the heart I was always useless and awkward. When I became blind it only added to my miserable dilemma. To make things worse the places I first went to, when I finally plucked up the courage to go, were, of course, nightclubs. At the time they were the perfect setting to meet sexy girls who had similar desires – but it would take six pints to pluck up the courage to ask any of them to dance.

They are done away with today but I have to admit, if it wasn't for the slow set I don't know how guys of my generation would have ever contemplated approaching girls. It was a good time for pulling in all honesty. If a girl danced with you the sky was the limit and today, even though it's not uncommon for a girl to approach a guy and the boundaries have changed slightly, they are still good places to go when you want to meet someone.

Picture the nightclub setting, however, when you are blind.

For a start, the night never looks as promising or exciting. If you pardon the pun it doesn't, in fact, look like anything at all but a dark vacuum with a lot of noise. For many reasons clubs must be among the hardest places on Earth for a visually impaired person to navigate, never mind contemplate pulling a chick within.

First of all it is impossible to make eye contact with the woman of your desires. While your friends are off pulling, you are left sitting looking into space not knowing if they are even sitting with you – and often they are not. Because of the noise you are left shouting without realising you are alone and communicating into thin air, looking like a right bollocks. And when you do finally get up on the dance floor it is usually with your several pals who form a protective circle around you in which to dance.

Well, this is the well-intentioned plan, but on a dance floor where inhibitions are lost to the frenzied rhythms of sexual energy the circle is often forgotten. More than once, in that case, one of my friends came to tear me away from a potentially embarrassing situation. One where I was sizing up and trying to impress, not a hot curvy lady but a cold brick wall – giving it the best smile I could muster.

At least I never asked the wall did it go there often!

*

So you can see my dilemma. It wasn't an easy time, but I got there in the end and it was all thanks to a wonderful lady I met in Torquay who came into my life and changed it around, if only briefly.

After a month of being under the military command of the former paratrooper who was my mobility officer, I was assigned to another more gentile one and although she did not impart the same wisdom and knowledge as my previous teacher, she left me with something even more precious. She gave me the gift of feeling human again by bringing a joy and passion to my life that I honestly believed I would never have.

Well one thing is for certain it was definitely not love at first sight!

But I warmed to her straight away as her laugh and bubbly energy were infectious. Our conversations just flowed and, despite her being twice my age, I felt far more comfortable than I did in the company of girls my own age, with whom conversations would often lapse into moments of extreme awkward silence. I was nineteen and, by then, knew that I was drawn to this woman because of her age and maturity as it enabled her to see beyond the blindness and discover the person within.

It was not that girls my own age where immature, but the baggage I was carrying was too heavy a weight for me to offload on a young woman who was just trying to find her own way in life. I felt I would be a burden and so I had made a conscious decision not to block any young woman's path in life or inflict myself upon them. I was knocked down on my own walk of life and I was damned if I was going to drag any young lady with me.

So, when I fell for my new teacher it was because she could see through

41

the immature doubts and mixed emotions that were violently rattling inside of me. And I soon found myself letting go, as I figured that I would not be a threat to her already established and steady path.

As a result she slowly but surely chipped away at the hard casing I had built up around myself and before I knew it I was head over heels. My shyness evaporated when I was with her and I can tell you, it might have been late in the losing, but by Christ it was worth it!

It was, of course, not one of my assigned modules. It was a beautiful gift and an exciting one that with some repetition I also mastered – without a white cane!

Remembering the moments I had with her brings a smile to my face as I can still hear her infectious laugh and feel her gentle touch. It was her air of confidence that constantly reassured me and made me feel almost invincible.

The weekend I stayed in her house it was as though the rest of the world did not exist and there were only the two of us reaching out to one another

Sadly, however, like all good things, my brief love affair came to an abrupt and decisive end. I say this because my mother decisively and abruptly ended it for me.

While on a visit to Britain my concerned sisters met the lady in question and were obviously not much impressed with the difference in age, so returned home with the full story. On receiving this information my mother, like all Irish mothers, sharpened her claws and tongue in preparation for battle. She then took the next flight out of Dublin to confront the jezebel who had stolen her vulnerable son's virtue.

This ridiculous conviction led to her engaging my unfortunate cougar and warning her, that if she didn't leave her son alone she would have no hesitation in going to the board of directors and demanding that they have her sacked for wrongful liaisons with a client.

In truth, however, it was me who vigorously exploited and took advantage of my older and more experienced companion. I may have been blind but certainly not vulnerable – not to the extent that my mother hoped I was, in this case anyway. I can safely, and joyously, say that this was one time in my life that I went into something with my eyes wide open, metaphorically speaking.

So even though she was not impressed with everything I had learned and achieved, my mother could not help but admire, and be encouraged by, the progress and obvious developed changes in the son that finally came home from Britain.

Chapter Thirteen

THE challenges I faced, while over in the UK, had built a momentum and pace within me that I quite liked. It was the stimulus I needed and a perfect distraction. Now that I was home I didn't want this roller coaster to slow down so I almost immediately applied for a guide dog.

Though quite efficient with the white cane, I just was not altogether happy with the slow pace I was reduced to when walking and the dog seemed the perfect solution. So following a successful interview with the association I was declared a perfect candidate for a dog. Not only that, I was also told that I would be the youngest owner of a guide dog in Ireland.

There are a number of vital elements required for the relationship between the owner and the guide dog to work and in the initial stages the instructor will actively seek similar traits or characteristics between the two future companions. The instructor can get an impression of what type of dog will suit by simply spending the day with the potential owner, asking various questions and basically finding out the type of environment the new dog could be entering into. By simply going for a walk with me he gauged my typical pace and estimated the height of dog that would be suitable for me. So with all this information at the organisation's disposal, I was curious and waited with intrepid anticipation to see what type of dog they would finally match me to.

The day could not come quick enough, but not just for me. Close friends and family were also anticipating my first encounter with my new four-legged friend.

It has been said to me by numerous people, some friends and others I may have had a brief encounter with along the way, that I'm not your typical blind person – whatever that is! I never challenged anyone on this insightful observation as I wasn't aware there was such a thing, but then I realised I had made the same assumption about my guide dog. There would be a standard and that's what I would receive…

This turned out to be very naïve of me and I realised this straight away the day that I met my, larger than life, dog Libby. I will never forget my first introduction with the golden retriever, as she literally jumped into my arms and smothered me with a big tongue of sloppy boisterous kisses – with no regard for the infuriated commands of her embarrassed instructor. My initial reaction was one of shock and my first thought was, had my interview, all those months ago, gone so terribly wrong that they would give me such a lunatic?

I was baffled and tried desperately to figure out what on earth I had said or done in my assessment interview for the organisation to conclude that I would be a perfect match for such a high-spirited creature. While my fellow students were introduced to their more docile and obedient dogs, one a German Shepherd and the other a Rhodesian Ridgeback, I could not help but feel that my Libby was going to prove a right madam – I wasn't wrong.

I knew I had a challenge on my hands from the moment I met her. I also knew that our personalities would combine to either implode or compliment and although I was sceptical I hoped for the latter, because in all honesty it was her sheer boldness that made me fall in love with her straight away.

There is a very good reason that I referred to Libby as a madam – that's the nickname she was given by one of the young ladies working in the kennels. The name stuck with her and it suited her in more ways than one. She actually responded to it quicker than ever she did when called Libby, and I quickly figured why. Any of the numerous times she would get up to mischief the staff would not reprimand her by shouting *LIBBY!* but rather *MADAM!* with the perfect sting in its pronunciation.

The first few days of training with my new dog were vital, as these were referred to as the bonding days where dog and owner gain a mutual trust and respect for each other. The way to make this happen, or to see if it was going to, was to have us, the owners, take our dogs everywhere we went.

We were actually told not to "let them out of our sight!" I think when the instructor gave this command he may have meant that we should not be out of the dog's sight, but nevertheless I took it quite seriously and that night I even brought Libby into the bathroom while I had a bath. This, however, proved unwise because while I was soaking in the tub we both dozed off into blissful sleep. Some time later I was pulled out of the depths of that sleep though, by a banging on the door. And before I could respond to it a startled Libby jumped up and immediately reacted by launching into the tub beside me!

If that was not bad enough I had forgotten to lock the door and the concerned person on the other side came in to find dog and owner splashing wildly in a scene of pure pandemonium. As I roared at Libby to get out of the bath, the young girl screamed in response to the horror of the situation and in her thick Cork accent then asked what on earth was going on?

"What the hell does it look like?" I roared. "LIIIBBBYYY!!! Get out!" I screamed, absolutely mortified.

With that, a frantic and confused Libby jumped out of the bath and into the unfortunate girl's arms, completely soaking her in the process. It became increasingly embarrassing for both of us, as she tried desperately to hold back a soaking Libby while I, in my humiliation, tried with little success to hide my shame – among other things.

What went through that young woman's mind I will never know, but at breakfast the following morning I was politely informed by my instructor, that I had taken the whole bonding with one's guide dog to a totally new level. The declaration was followed up with a chorus of laughter and sniggers from everyone present, and my mortification was complete.

*

I have often heard that there is always one dog, in a litter of pups, who is considered the runt. If this is the case then Libby was certainly the runt in hers. Mischievous and stubborn she absolutely fit the bill, and although it was difficult at times there was never a dull moment.

I experienced this on the first morning I began my outdoor training with her in a small estate on the fringes of Cork city. There was nothing too difficult the first day as the task was just for me to familiarise myself walking side by side with her while holding onto the harness. Simple enough you might say, and so it should have been but before I continue I would like to clear up a few misconceptions about guide dogs and what they are capable of doing. They are not, as is often assumed, capable of acknowledging and distinguishing between the different colours of the traffic lights. On the contrary – it is up to the handler to figure out when it is safe to cross the road. It is the dog's ability to simply find the lights and guide the handler safely across by avoiding any obstacles that might be on the path to the other side.

Another huge misconception is that the owner has little or nothing to do but tell the dog where he or she desires to go and the dog miraculously takes him or her there. On observation it may look like the dog is supernatural – but trust me this is not the case. The dog is by no means a sat nav that can be programmed with the push of a few buttons. Of course, that would be a fantastic concept but the reality is that the handler needs to be aware at all times where he or she is geographically. Then, with a few simple commands and a particular tone of voice, the dog (more often than not) will obey and bring the owner safely to his/her destination.

The primary job of the dog is to avoid the numerous obstacles on the way to almost anywhere and the time when this is particularly paramount, and there is no room for mistakes, is when it comes to what is referred to as off kerb obstacles. This is an obstacle that is obstructing the entire path and consequently dog and owner cannot get past. The only alternative is for the dog to guide the owner to the edge of the path as close to the obstruction as possible. When there is no oncoming traffic the command will be given for the dog to find the way onto the road, staying as close to the edge as possible, and then immediately back up onto the path as soon as the obstacle has been maneuvered around.

It was around the third day when the terrain became more difficult and Libby decided to show her true colours, determined to show who was top dog. It had become a battle of wills and like any blossoming relationship the course of our true love didn't run smooth. It wasn't one thing in particular, she just seemed to go against me on everything. It was so bad that I had decided that if she continued to play up continuously, I was going to get the hell out of Cork and as far away as possible from that irritating little bitch.

It was for this very reason my instructor gently took me aside and gave me an insight into the psychology of dogs, and my stubborn madam in particular. It proved a revelation. Putting it simply, he told me that Libby, being a pack animal, saw me as part of the pack and wanted dominance over me. It was because of her innate intelligence she was testing me at every opportunity. It was, therefore, up to me to show her I was boss and to, under no circumstances, give in because she would exploit this weakness and slowly but surely break down my resolve.

Apparently Libby's unique and stubborn attributes were similar to those which I had in abundance. It was, therefore, my relentless stubbornness and willpower that made Libby into the super intelligent dog she eventually proved to be.

By not giving in to her deliberate mistakes, but instead tirelessly correcting them with constant repetition to the point of exhaustion, I finally won her over. And once we'd gained a mutual respect, trust and love for one another our working relationship and friendship took on a momentum all of its own – and we were unstoppable.

Chapter Fourteen

NOW, I'm not saying it was all plain sailing throughout the years that followed – there were times Libby tried my patience almost to breaking point and, I admit, there were times I gave in and she won.

There was the time, shortly after I came home from Cork, and I was practicing a particular route, that I knew I would be using quite frequently, with her. Within a week of constant repetition we had the journey memorised and down to such a fine art, that I can boastfully say it was pure perfection. While taking the same route about a week or so later, however, Libby decided to have one of her stubborn fits. Everything was going smoothly right up to the point where she came to a fork in the road. I gave her the command to turn left, which was the routine at this junction, but she refused to move a step further. Thinking there was an obstruction on the path I made an allowance for her obstinacy. With careful investigation, however, I realised that there was no obstacle and the only conclusion I could draw was that my darling Libby was having one of her stubborn moments. So with all the authority I could muster I demanded she turn left.

But I could not budge her from her defiant stance.

Most dogs would jump at such an order – not my Libby though. My mother often commented that if I could only see the facial expressions of her when I gave out to her, they would turn me to stone. When madam was reprimanded harshly, she would not react with swift obedience but the exact opposite. She would literally plonk herself flat out on the ground and Saint Francis himself, the talker of animals, could not have budged her.

This was one of those days and after switching from swearing, to cajoling, to words of endearment and back to swearing, nothing would get my beloved dog to shift. I had no other choice so, but to backtrack on our route and come to my destination from a different direction.

Needless to say she repeated the very same symptom the following day.

I say symptom as I was half convinced there was something psychologically wrong with the dog. I knew it was nothing physical because that very evening I took her to the vet who gave her the all clear. The vet was no dog whisperer though so, unfortunately, I got no insight into Libby's state of mind.

I figured I was to struggle through this puzzle myself and sure enough the answer became apparent the following day, and it turned out to be no big mystery whatsoever.

As I mentioned Libby would stop at a fork in the road and refuse to budge when given the command to turn left. This day, however, I decided to give her the command to turn right, and with that the tail started wagging with delight. All she wanted was to get the better of me with her own way. She was tired of doing the same route over and over and simply wanted a change of scenery. I was disgusted, but relieved at the same time that we were moving forward again.

The situation, however, became a force of habit throughout the following years and, as we were a team, I would often give in to her inquisitive and nosey manner and allow myself to be taken on adventures that would prove challenging and exciting, even for me.

It is indescribable the precious freedom and independence I obtained thanks to my partnership with Libby and her eagerness to learn new routes because it kept me on my toes. Her intelligence was infectious and within a month we had more or less mastered my home area of Tallaght.

*

I would be lying if I did not say I was more than nervous the day I decided to venture into Dublin city centre. It was the first time since I lost my sight that I would be taking such a trip unaccompanied, apart from my dog. My mother, in vain, tried to insist that my sister tag along with me, but after a lot of yelling then invoking all the angels and saints, and anything else that may have been listening, to watch over me, she relented.

I was never so proud of my precious Libby as I was that day and it soon became clear that the more challenging and demanding a route was for her, the better. Another amazing quality that I discovered she had was the incredible gift of attracting the opposite sex.

When I say this I don't mean hers but, fantastically, mine. She was most definitely a babe magnet and if I didn't know better I would have sworn she was trained in gaining the attention of young attractive women. Not that I complained, but I had to abide by the strict cardinal rules of the guide dog association, and that is not to allow the general public pet the dog while in harness and working.

This proved, on some occasions, to be a huge distraction for dog and owner and the only thing to do was to give in and let the lady, or ladies, in question manhandle my dog.

On this day, our first in the city centre, a young lady approached me while I was waiting to cross the road and politely asked if I needed her assistance. "Excuse me sir, but would you like to cross the road?"

No, I am just standing here for the good of my health I thought, insulted at first.

"Yes, please," I replied, despite this, because how could I refuse such warm generosity?

It was obvious from her accent that she was a Yank and as she took my arm it was quite evident that she was tall, almost as tall as me, and had an air of confidence that only Yanks possess. I would like to think it was my devilish good looks that grabbed her attention, but unfortunately it was not.

"Oh my God, you have such a handsome dog," she squealed as she stopped to pet Libby.

Somewhat pissed with this attention I proceeded to walk away, when she asked; "So are you going anywhere in particular? I could walk with you a bit further if you like?"

This was music to my ears.

"No," was my reply. "Just out for a ramble."

"Well, I have time to kill before my next lecture, so would you like to catch a coffee with me?"

You bloody marvel I thought about Libby as I casually replied; "Sure why not? I have anything else to do."

And as she slid her arm into mine we both fell into easy conversation.

"So where are you studying?" I asked.

"Trinity college."

"Nice. So do you like Ireland?"

"I love it." You could practically hear her smiling.

"So what is it you like, exactly?" I laughed.

"Oh, the night life is wonderful and you Irish are just marvellous."

"You think so?" I was intrigued.

"Most definitely."

What a stroke of luck I thought. *This day could not get any better.*

All of a sudden, however, I heard someone call my name from behind. I say someone but I knew straight away that it was the unmistakable tone of my big sis, who was now urgently shouting out my name.

"Robert, hey, wait up it's me Loreena!"

Pretending not to hear her and hoping to get lost in the bustling crowds, proved futile as moments later she caught up and was walking alongside of my new acquaintance and me. Introducing herself as no less than my "big sis," she was totally oblivious to my sheer disgust and downright annoyance.

"So I take it you are Robert and this is your sister?" said the Yank, with what I hoped was a hint of disappointment in her tone.

"Yes," was all I could muster, the notion of going for coffee now abandoned.

"I guess we won't be doing coffee right now then?"

"I suppose not."

I felt like a child, but I was seething with my sister and my mother and in fairness I doubted this lovely lady would want to be in my company any

49

longer anyway. So, with some reluctance, I bid her farewell.

I know I should not have been pissed off with my sister, who was only obeying the orders of my overly-concerned mother, but at that point I was incapable of rational thought, so I ignored her throughout the entire awkward bus journey home.

As I sit here bringing Libby back to life, if only in my memories, it is with deep joy and gratitude that I recollect the precious years I had with her. She unconditionally gave so much of her life to me. She was a loveable rogue, with a mind totally of her own and this is what I loved most about her.

Another quality of mine that she had was a lack of patience and there were many times she displayed this to such great capacity, that I would end up losing mine. If she had to sit and behave for any extended period of time boredom would take over and, like a spoilt child, she would throw a tantrum by stamping her two front feet, demanding to be taken home.

When her outbursts failed madam, on occasion, cunningly chewed through her lead and I would not be made aware of what she had done until it was pointed out to me that my darling was making her way towards the door.

Once she managed this trick while I was in the middle of an exam in college. Chewing through her lead again she managed to make her way out of the building and over to a nearby field.

Because the outdoors she loved and there was one passion both of us most definitely shared – this was our love of hill walking. She would love nothing better than running carelessly through the heather, or better still, a wet and murky bog, and she had a talent for choosing the filthiest parts of the bog before lunging head first into the black thick of it.

There is one walk in particular that stands out in my memory as it was challenging, not just for Libby and me, but also for two very good friends of mine. The walk, or correctively putting it, trek, was climbing to the summit of the highest mountain in the British Isles – Ben Nevis in the Highlands of Scotland.

Chapter Fifteen

BEN Nevis was my first serious climb, and it carved a trail to my heart and a passion in me to pursue other famous mountains throughout the world, afterwards.

That trek was the one and only time Libby accompanied me on such a trip and, unlike me, she had no trepidation whatsoever. Mind you, she wasn't dying with a mountainous hangover after over-indulging in the highland beer the night before, either!

If not verbally, Libby certainly chastised us with her looks of contempt and barks of disgust that morning. With no consideration for our self-inflicted suffering, she tackled the mountain with great bursts of speed and agility, only to turn every few minutes and give us a high-pitched bark that signalled her increasing impatience.

Throughout the walk, my friends threatened to throw my "irritating beast" off the mountain, along with me for bringing her. It was only on the descent, that their attitude changed towards Libby when they noticed she was beginning to struggle navigating some of the bigger rocks. It was apparent that she had spent all her energy on the climb and was, at that stage, tired.

The hike had taken well over eight hours to complete, and both man and beast were quite content when floundering towards the final stretch to reach civilisation. But just as we were reaching the bottom Libby noticed a river nearby and before any of us were aware of her intention she managed to develop a burst of new energy. Like a dog possessed, she ran and blindly jumped straight into the freezing water.

The panicked shouts from my friends were almost instantaneous as they frantically watched Libby being washed downstream in the strong current. "Oh fucking hell," screamed Tony.

"What's wrong?" I asked, now panicked myself.

"That mad dog of yours is just after jumping into the river and is been washed away!"

My heart felt like it stopped for a moment, as I imagined my precious Libby frightened and drowning.

"What do you mean?" I shouted, desperate for an answer. But I didn't get one as both men left me standing on my own in sheer bewilderment. Without hesitation, and with no regard for their own safety, both friends dived in, fully clothed, to rescue my stricken dog.

As they drew closer, I was later informed, Libby turned on hearing her name and noticed them gaining on her. I can only assume she reckoned it was some sort of game, because to my mates' dismay she suddenly, and effortlessly, began to paddle faster before circling right around them and making her way back to the far side of the bank. There, she gracefully glided out of the water and moments later turned back around before leaping in again and swimming out to her new-found playmates.

When the three eventually emerged, Libby seemed to have been given a new lease of life and she boldly and casually walked up the bank of the river, before shaking her coat dry.

I could not, however, say the same for my friends.

I was hoping, before they managed to sludge their way up the embankment that Libby and I could miraculously disappear, but no such luck. And for the first time since losing my sight, I was somewhat thankful I could not see them – the sound of their silence was enough!

Chapter Sixteen

RELIGION was never a subject I found particularly interesting, so the day two young men called Mark and Damien, walked into our classroom of fifth year students to talk about it, I was most likely daydreaming. Shortly after their arrival, however, the men, who appeared to be in their late twenties and from Northern Ireland, got our attention.

First off they had an unmistakable air of authority in their voices, but even more evident was the air of conviction and unashamed truth. They did not mince words as they told us that both had served time in prison for being involved with paramilitary organisations. The guy doing most of the talking, Damien, informed us that he had been a high-ranking member of the INLA, were Mark was a former member of the IRA.

You could have heard a pin drop in the room as every student, ear cocked, hung on every word of the two. None of us, however, were prepared when their topic of conversation took a totally unexpected and extremely different direction. After describing some of the horrors and violence they both witnessed and perpetrated, the story became a testimony of how their lives were dramatically changed while serving a stretch in the notorious Long Kesh Prison. It became somewhat surreal when both began to explain how they were miraculously changed from bitter and hateful men, to men of peace and forgiveness.

This dramatic change they stated, was due to the direct intervention and spiritual enlightenment of the almighty himself.

If my words sound a bit cynical that is because at seventeen years of age their revelations sounded, to me, like a load of bullshit.

They claimed, that while in prison, they became friendly with the Chaplin that resided over it. At the time of their incarceration there was something happening of great magnitude in a little country village in the foothills of Bosnia Herzegovina. The same priest told them of this village known as Medjugorje, and how the Virgin Mary had appeared to several young children there. They believed the priest to be totally off his head and were actually annoyed at how he dared speak of such nonsense when all they cared about was revolution. It even became a battle of theirs, almost a personal vendetta, to oppose this man and all he represented.

So they challenged him on everything and over time he revealed to them the details of the strange phenomena in Medjugorje; and although they mocked him they kept going back to him wanting to know more.

Damien described to the class, how his determined anger mysteriously turned to curiosity and for some unknown reason he began to read the messages that the Virgin Mary was bestowing on these visionaries, to reveal to the world.

While sitting in the class listening to these men describe their lives having been turned upside down by these messages that the mother of God was, supposedly, giving to some kids in a far off land, I was thinking one thing. These guys reckoned my classmates and I were gullible fools and had concocted this elaborate story as a means to walking away from their troubled past. What did peak my interest, however, was the fact that they were hoping to start a prayer group in the girls' secondary school across the field from our own school barracks, and shortly after that initial meeting myself and a friend decided to drop in to the new group.

Thinking only of the opportunity to meet girls, I swaggered in, half intoxicated and completely unaware that it would be a night that would evolve into something much bigger, and in later days take my life down a road that would change it forever.

I remember how I unashamedly joined in their songs of adoration and praise while we sat in a tight circle, within which was a statue of the Virgin Mary. It was with fits of giggles, influenced by the consumption of alcohol, that my friend and I sang too loud and totally out of tune.

The reason we were slightly tipsy was because we had attended a soccer match earlier that day, where Ireland miraculously beat Spain in an unforgettable game. Now if that was not a miracle I don't know what is! Regardless of Ireland's huge achievement, however, my celebratory behaviour was inexcusable and I admit I was a downright ass that night. So it surprised me, at the end of the night, when the two former Republicans made their way across the room to chat to my friend and me.

"So, what about ye guys?" Damien, in his unmistakable accent, asked.

"Not much," I mumbled, not so confident all of a sudden.

"I know your face," he said to me then.

Oh fuck I thought as fear crawled up my spine, *how does this guy recognise my face?*

"No, you couldn't," came my reply.

"No, I never forget a face," he insisted.

That's his bloody IRA training I thought to myself.

"Ah, yes," he continued. "I remember now. You are one of the lads from the college across the way. So how was the match?"

"The match?" I was confused for a minute. "Oh grand." I could feel myself relax a little.

Having a conversation with these two guys felt weird as I was half expecting them to drag the two of us outside and, if not kneecap us at least beat the living daylights out of us for our rude interruption and disrespect.

The total opposite is how we were treated though, as they greeted us with genuine warmth and sincerity and; despite my alcohol haze, I was touched. Eventually they both asked me if I would be coming back the following week.

I can vividly remember walking home that night, through the local park in the pitch dark, humming one of the songs the group was singing earlier that night.

That prayer group soon became the highlight of my week, because to me it was so much more. Indeed the girls there were beautiful, but I can honestly say that they were no longer the only reason for my attendance. There was camaraderie among the group that is hard to put into words, but suffice to say, for the first time I felt I could be myself, without all the false bullshit that comes with being a teenager, within a group of people.

Nobody there was trying to prove anything, and what I loved the most about the group was the genuine friendships that grew as we openly shared our baggage without embarrassment or judgement. I came to know Mark and Damien really well. They openly talked about their experiences in the troubles at home and their involvement in them. You could not help but be touched by their anguish and pain when they recollected their former life, and when they began to talk about Medjugorje, it was the weirdest thing because a wonderful entity seemed to transcend over them and they became different people.

I began to understand how they first felt when challenging the Chaplin during their stretch in prison, because like them I constantly wanted to challenge them and contradict them in an effort to find some flaw in what they claimed. But though I made it my mission to see through their false talk and penetrate their armour, I soon discovered with scary revelation, that the only armour to be found was the one I was wearing.

Like them, I began to listen to the messages of Medjugorje and they became very important to me – but it was to be a while before their true relevance, for me, would come to light.

Chapter Seventeen

I HOPE I'm not creating an image or making these two guys out to be some sort of weird holy freaks. If this is the image I have created, or it's what you may be thinking, delete it out of your head straight away as it is the furthest thing from the truth.

If anything they were two ordinary lads who could get up to great devilment and party and have the craic as much as anyone – or even better. The only difference in these guys was that when you looked at them, and I mean really looked at them, you knew they had been to hell and back; but found peace thanks to some little town in the foothills of Bosnia Herzegovina.

I can categorically state that the prayer group was far from being on bended knee and praying all the time, as I recall the nights we would hang out in the lads' flat in Rathmines. Though not all that crazy, I'm sure the good lady of heaven would have frowned at some of the antics we managed to get up to.

I'm sure Mark and Damien had varying reasons, and deep personal ones, for starting up the prayer group, known in-house as the God Squad, but their main objective was to get members to Medjugorje. This undertaking was to involve a considerable amount of fundraising that proved to be quite challenging and even, on occasion, slightly embarrassing for a teenager. I was often the red-faced boy seen on Grafton Street banging a drum, while people threw money in our baskets – but I got on with it.

I really wanted to make it to this holy land and either lay my scepticism to rest or get on board with the holy elements. Either way, I had decided, when I finally got there, I was going to have a good time.

I never got to see the magnificent beauty of Medjugorje though, not with my eyes anyway, because as luck would have it, it around this time my world cruelly took another path – into complete darkness.

When my sight was ripped from me, the last thing on my mind was some village a million miles from the crushing reality that then presented itself and, as I figured God had abandoned me so too did I, the God Squad.

Little did I know though, that they would not abandon me.

*

One night while my family and I were sitting in the living room, we heard a commotion outside.

What on earth?" said my mother puzzled, as she made her way to the window.

There was a sharp intake of breath and I could hear the music, louder and louder.

"Robert, come here," she said.

"For what?"

"Just come here."

Joining her at the window, but of course not being able to see, just hear what was going on, I felt her hand on my arm.

"It's your friends from the prayer group," she said, an audible lump in her throat.

I didn't know what to think but I didn't have much time as she went out to greet them and they insisted on having a prayer meeting in my house.

Meeting the gang for the first time since my accident, there was none of the awkward silence that I initially received from some of my other friends, and I immediately felt that air of kinship. Inwardly my pain was still tearing me up, but I could not help but be affected by the group's love and compassion, which burrowed a little hole into my heart that night as a few tears formed around my freshly-dead eyes. What was also infectious that night was the group's excited anticipation about finally going to Medjugorje, that August for the world youth festival. I tried not to show my disappointment as I knew whatever plan was in store for me then, it certainly was not going to be abroad with them.

So you could say I was a little shocked some days later, when out of the blue, my mother casually asked me how I would like to go to Medjugorje that May. She told me that she had been talking to Damien and it was he who suggested I should go with my parents as he would be working over there at the time as a tour guide and could easily take the time to look after us.

Why not? I reckoned. If nothing else the break was desperately needed.

So with the decision made both parents and I decided to take two weeks holidays, spending one week in Medjugorje, and the other on the magnificent beaches of Split along the Adriatic Coast.

*

It was quite odd when Damien met us at the airport in Dubrovnik and informed us, along with about forty other pilgrims, that he was to be our host and guide for the week. While he led into the rosary on the bus I grinned to myself with the thought; *If only the rest of the people on this bus knew of this man's background, would they be so willing to pray with him?*

I remember the bus struggling with the twists and turns as it made its endless climb up into the mountains and I think the people were really silently praying for the driver to navigate the bends safely and get us all to our destination in one piece. It was dark, so many were in a similar boat to myself, unable to see much, and I too could be heard uttering the Lord's name throughout the journey – just not in prayer!

It was early in the morning when we finally arrived in the mountainous village, were we were quickly dispatched to our residence. A family home, which myself and my parents were to share with the owners for the week. This was my first surprise, as I half thought we would be staying in a hotel. I wasn't expecting anything luxurious, but a hotel nonetheless.

I felt a bit humbled when meeting the family of the house as it was almost two in the morning and their hospitality and warmth was so sincere. Though the house was a typical country residence and nothing too lavish, there was a beautiful homely feeling about it and the lady of it, with little or no English, managed to portray her warmth perfectly. Her two daughters did the talking for me while my dad informed me of their complexions, and little else, on my persistent request.

They had the same genuine warmth of their mother emanating from them, but one in particular I took to straight away. *Maybe this pilgrimage is not going to be too bad after all*, I thought later, as I fell into an exhausted sleep.

To my annoyance the village wakes up very early and pilgrims doing sacrifice on these trips tend to have this one as the first of the day.

I was greeted by Damien outside the main church at around 9am.

"So what about you mucker? he asked, as he greeted me with a bear hug. "Not much, what about you?" I asked, not really caring.

I was barely awake as he informed me that he had already climbed the mountain known as Krizevac and so I was barely listening, as the heat of the morning was gathering momentum. All that was going through my mind, as he enthusiastically described the stations of the cross on the mountain, which run right up to the summit where the cross of Jesus stands looking down over the whole village, was that this guy was slightly mad.

My father, the confessed atheist, was like me that morning and only half listening were my mother, God bless her, was like Damien and already caught up in the spiritual frenzy.

*

That evening Damien brought his group of pilgrims to one of the houses from which one of the visionaries made a speech. A few hundred devoted faithful gathered outside this woman's house in the sweltering heat to listen to her proclaim her miraculous encounter with the Virgin Mary.

People stood in rapturous silence as she described what the lady of heaven looked like, and the messages she wanted to give to the world. I listened, but her words did not penetrate me.

That night Damien took us to a local bar where my father received plenty of the spirit through a variety of liquors. This got him into a heated debate with Damien and my mother as he announced his total disbelief and questioned the gullible natures of the pilgrims travelling to Medjugorje.

During the silent walk home that night I think my mother was offering up a few prayers in recompense for my father's misguided and lost soul.

The following day being Friday there was great anticipation in the village, as this was the day that the Virgin Mary gave her weekly apparition to all the visionaries on the mountain – known as Apparition Mountain, but Mt Podbrdo to locals. I was in two minds as to whether I would trek up the mountain that night but curiosity got the better of me. Mind you, when the heavens later opened, and not with angels or anything else as spectacular, I was inwardly praying that the visionaries would give us a message that Our Lady was calling off the visit.

There was to be no such luck though, as my family, I, and hundreds of excited worshippers, who seemed oblivious to the torrential downpour, began to make their way up the mountain. If the blasted rain was not bad enough, it made the getting there much more difficult as you could imagine thousands of feet all going in the same direction and ultimately creating a path of sloppy sludge and mud.

Rocks and boulders also needed to be navigated, so the going was extremely tough and it wasn't just me that slipped a few times. Many other people were finding the terrain just as dangerous as they slipped and fell around me.

If this is what is meant by sacrifice I want out, I thought.

All I wanted to do was turn around and make my way back to a bar to have a few cold, wet beers. Typically, when we finally reached the top, and I was strategically placed on a rock close to the visionaries, it suddenly stopped raining.

If only the apparition could have been called off for another hour I cursed to myself.

While sitting there wet and freezing, the worshippers began to pray, chat and softly sing in many different languages, again seemingly oblivious to their discomfort. All I was feeling was my backside killing me and I wondered if Damien couldn't have picked a smoother rock for me to sit on. After about half an hour of praying and singing, there was a sudden hush over the congregation as though a silent trance fell over them. I assumed this was around the moment that Our Lady was going to appear to the visionaries and that was the reason for the sudden calm.

Up to then I had been a cynic, a doubting Thomas, and if I'm honest I really couldn't have cared less, so what happened to me next I swear to you is no exaggeration or figment of my imagination.

While sitting on the rock I began to feel very uneasy. I just wanted out of there and I even began to panic. In the same instance I, for no apparent reason, began to rock back and forward. I tried to control this and make my body stop. I even tried to command it to stop, but could not. It was then I felt a strange presence wash over me and invade my whole being and as I was trying to fight it, the voice inside me kept repeating itself with the gentle words, *let it go, let it go.*

And as I sat there I began to give into the fight raging inside of me and I literally felt all my anger, resentment and sadness being taken from me. This was replaced with a tremendous love, peace and calm.

Now you may ask what on Earth this was. Was it divine intervention?

I asked this in the months that followed and came up with the truth being that whatever held me in her arms that night was all powerful and not of this Earth; and when I gave into my inner battle this divine love washed over me and took my pain away.

I came off the mountain that night a different man, in so many ways, and it was quite evident afterwards in my whole being, and attitude.

The change in me was so apparent that I think the real miracle that occurred was the fact that my father, the total atheist, went to confession the following morning.

Chapter Eighteen

WHEN I went home friends and family commented on the change that had taken place in me. They remarked on how happy I was and said I seemed more relaxed and at peace with myself and my life.

That August I did manage to go out again to Medjugorje with the prayer group, and this time my big sis accompanied me. She was fighting her own personal battle and finding it hard to accept that God would leave me blind. She was quite angry when I had come home the previous May and could not reconcile with the fact that I had somehow accepted my predicament with a more calmer and different outlook.

She was half expecting me to arrive home having been miraculously cured of my blindness, not my inner conflict.

Her argument was, if God wanted to cure me, why do it in half measure? Why not go the whole way and give me back my sight?

I am not going to say what happened my sister, Loreena, in Medjugorje, but like most of the God Squad that went over there she was also touched by something miraculous and not of this Earth; and it gave her the peace and wisdom to let go of her inner turmoil.

*

Like most major changes in life or events that tend to shape us, nine times out of ten it is as though they are preordained and circumstance leads you to the next thing.

Not long after this time I joined an organisation known as Blind Sports, which catered for a variety of different sports players – but the one I got involved with was running.

I never considered or realised how out of shape I was until I began to run with other visually impaired participants. And soon I decided to concentrate all my efforts on the 100 metre sprint, thinking it would be easy enough. In comparison to my fellow athletes, I was superbly unfit, but I was also determined not to come in last every time, which spurred me on.

While panting for breath on one occasion, I overheard a conversation that two of the visually impaired were having. At first I thought my ears were deceiving me, as they talked openly about going to Austria to compete in, no less than, mountain skiing. To my fascination, they informed me that a bunch of visually impaired and fully-sighted people would be spending a week in Austria in the famous ski resort of San Johann.

I could scarcely believe it and bombarded them with questions. I was fascinated and soon decided that this was certainly a challenge I would be up for. It would beat running around a field any day.

And so, it was the start of the first adventure of many that would take me around the world while fundraising for the National Council for the Blind of Ireland.

Before we were to embark upon our trip to Austria, it was requested that we all practiced on a dry slope in the foothills of the Wicklow Mountains. This was a great opportunity to meet all the gang going and also reassured our Irish ski instructors that we would not kill ourselves, or anyone else, on the slopes as we practiced for the real thing.

I remember the first time I was introduced to my ski instructor, Kathleen, and thinking to myself, *who is the crazy one here, me or her?*

"So, I take it you have never skied before?" she asked.

"You're dead right and I must be mad for ever trying to take it up," I replied.

"You will be grand. Sure we are going to take it nice and easy first time out," she reassured me.

"That's fine by me," I said, not believing a word of it.

Starting on the nursery slope and standing sideways towards the downhill Kathleen helped me put my skis on. So far so good, I reckoned.

Then she told me to face downhill, directing the points of my skis together and widening them apart at the back.

What could be so hard about this? I thought.

The tips kept crossing over each other, but when I had finally accomplished the stance I was told that was the first and the most important lesson for beginners because that position, known as snow plough, would be the one to help me to stop. After that, knees in tight and bent slightly, I was shown how to push into my boots, bring the back of the skis closer and set off down the slope.

Yippy!! I thought to myself, as I went flying down the nursery slope, ecstatic… but totally forgetting Kathleen's instruction about the snow plough and stopping, until I heard her at the top of her voice screaming "Stop, stop! Jesus stop!"

Falling on the dry slope was quite sore, mildly putting it, but I reckoned if I could put up with a few hard knocks and bruises on a hard slope full of brush-like bristles I would be well able for the soft powdery slopes of Austria – either way, nothing was going to stop me.

It was with a feeling of great triumph that I listened, as I was told later that day, that my skiing was a lot better than my big sis. I had tormented her, my uncle Aidan and my friend Thomas to come on the trip of a lifetime too.

It was out on the slopes of Kilternan that I met the man who was the coordinator of the fundraising trip too. He is a larger than life character in more ways than one, and I say that with genuine warmth and gratitude, as this man was the instigator of many more trips that I would be fortunate enough to go on.

Big Eamon (who was the size of at least three rugby players and had the tenacity of five Bob Geldoffs), as he is known, has a gift that makes you feel, when in his company, you are all important, and his skilful charm is so overpowering that he could convince you to do almost anything for him. Putting it bluntly, he would be capable of charming Mother Theresa into a strip club, and then convincing her she liked it.

In the years that followed our initial meeting, I was to hear many of Eamon's inspiring speeches where one moment he would bring tears to your eyes and the next have you in fits of laughter. I didn't always agree with the man, or some of his methods when it came to his campaigning and raising money for the NCBI; and there was times our friendship was quite fragile, but regardless of how we agreed or disagreed, I had tremendous respect for him and I do believe he held me in the same regard.

I'm sure anyone reading this, who has any interest in politics is quite aware of another character, who is also larger than life and a great man – David Norris. He too was part of the trip and not the only celebrity, with Davy Arthur, from the famous ballad band *Finbar Fury and Davy Arthur*, also travelling with us.

*

After a crazy week of sleepless nights and shenanigans it was Eamon who came up with the cardinal law that whatever happened on the trip stayed on trip, and even though I took the pledge I'm sure a few stories won't hurt!

What happens off the slopes is, I think, referred to as April skiing and there was quite a lot of that. This started promptly at 3pm every afternoon in the bar at the bottom of the slope, and those who were sober enough to walk would finish back in the bar in the town – or sometimes continue until it was time to go skiing the following morning.

There were a few occasions that the owners of one or two bars were so chuffed to have the famous Davy Arthur on their premises, that the sessions would actually go on to the small hours of the morning and right up to breakfast. And it wasn't just Davy that entertained, there were many other talented personalities on the trip that, with a few inside of them, had no inhibitions about performing musically.

Without hesitation I can honestly put my hand on my heart and say that my mate Tom is by far one of the greatest guitarists I have ever heard, and his talents had revellers dancing on tables many a night, while Davy himself sat mesmerised by him.

So, by day we mastered the slopes of Austria like we had been doing it all our lives and by night we were broken up into groups and given a challenge, where we would compete against each other. The night of the talent competition the Austrian spectators were left flushed and somewhat embarrassed as David Norris' team re-enacted a famous scene from Ulysses.

Then there was the competition I was put out by, or should I say, literally put out of. This was the one where a man and woman from each team had to go into the steam rooms together, without a stitch of clothing on – and when I say not a stitch I mean that. After spending so many minutes in the hot room they then had to go out and roll in the snow. Like most of the guys who were up for this, I certainly was as I figured, sure how the hell would I get embarrassed? I couldn't see a thing, including any woman or even myself! The women, however, decided that under no circumstances was I to compete in this little frolic because they all assumed that though I could not see, I would make up for this slight handicap by using my hands!

I will say no more!

*

The instructor who was assigned to me was, without exaggeration, about seventy. I remember while walking with him to the ski lift on the first day that his movement was very slow and thinking to myself, *this old fart must be riddled with Arthritis.*

I could not help but also notice, to my annoyance, that some of the other visually impaired were assigned to gorgeous Austrian bombshells.

Did I envy them as I made my way up the slope, on the lift, with my old dinosaur? Of course I did! But you know the saying, never judge a book by its cover and I should have reminded myself of this from the off, because I was very wrong.

About halfway up the mountain he informed me that there was where we were to get off and begin our first lesson.

"Now, Robert, we will begin very gently. Today I just want to see what you are capable of before we go higher up the mountain."

If we go any higher, I thought, *it will take half the day for this antique to come off the slope.*

"Now, I am going to ski in front of you," he continued, "holding out a pole in each hand, and you will hold from behind."

"Yep, sure, that's grand," I replied in my arrogance, eager to get going and hoping to go unnoticed, so embarrassed was I by my slope companion.

"Are you ready for the ride of your life?" he asked, oblivious to my shame.

"Yep, whatever," I wanted to say, but I simply muttered, "Ah, sure why not?"

A walk in the park I figured, sure this old relic was struggling to put his skis on for God's sake. And for a swift second I thought someone else had taken the polls in his place as we shot off down the mountain, because whoever it was it could not have been my toothless instructor.

If it was him, by Christ, he had suddenly become possessed with what I don't know, maybe it was all that fresh mountain air, but he had miraculously transformed into Evil Knievel on skis.

We tore down the mountain with an amazing speed and agility that left me holding onto the polls for dear life. Not only was this man in total control of the mountain as we twisted and turned, but he was in total control of me – his strength was so magnificently powerful that it was he, and he alone, that kept me upright.

Fuck me! I thought as I got to the bottom of the hill, breathless and shaking.

"You were right, that was the ride of my life!" I said.

Laughing, he simply replied, "I take it you have not met an Austrian woman yet."

If anything the freedom of the slopes was just what I wanted and I couldn't get enough of the speed and reckless abandonment that it gave me. I was on a magnificent high, right up until the third day were I literally came crashing, stumbling and falling back to reality.

I had, at that stage, progressed to what is referred to as the blue run, and I was quite happy with myself, and what I had mastered over the previous three days. I was quite familiar with the slope and it wasn't too strenuous, as each time we skied to the bottom of the slope we got on a chair lift and repeated the same one again.

I had not ventured off this slope and was quite comfortable with the speed and rhythm I had mastered. I felt fearless, invincible and more alive than I had in a long time. I felt I could do anything, which was a great thing as it was on this day that word reached me that the Gerry Ryan show – one of the biggest radio shows in Ireland, which was on the trip as an outside broadcast – wanted to interview me…right then!

There was nothing else for us to do but ski all the way down to the bottom of the mountain, and we had less than twenty minutes to do so. That ski run I will never forget because if I thought the old man was fast the first day, it was nothing compared to the frantic and scary trip he took me on at that moment. I had trusted him totally up to then, but the speed we went that time was even too much for me and I knew if I let go of the polls or stumbled I was a goner.

I recall whizzing past my sis, and the crowd she was with, as they shouted their hellos. I could barely make out their remarks of astonished disbelief as I flew past them and they gasped *holy shit!* and *holy fuck, is that Robert?*

Again I was totally safe, as at all times my amazing instructor was in total control, but flying down the mountain at breakneck speed it was hard to convince myself of this. So I can tell you now it was with a brandy in one hand and a cigarette in the other, that fifteen minutes later I was being interviewed by the well loved and sadly missed, Gerry Ryan.

I was well prepared for the questions Gerry asked me, and I talked about the tremendous freedom skiing gave me and the realisation of how fast I was going when I would hit a bump or little jump on the snow.

However, I don't think he was prepared for me, or the nation for that matter, when I went on to describe the carry on in the steam rooms and the competition in which I was cruelly and deliberately left out. I had Gerry in convulsions of laughter as I told him the reasons for this, but I also went on to mention that my big sister Loreena was one of the participants who volunteered to parade naked in the steam room and then proceed to frolic in the snow. I told the nation at home, how she was making a show of me as that was only half of some of the stuff she was getting up to and she was certainly not a good ambassador over there in Austria.

After the interview I received rapturous applause and the response and feedback from the listeners was equally positive. I cannot say I received the same reaction when Loreena heard of my mischief and it was at least two to three days before she came around and saw the funny side of things.

A week later, however, after her first day back in work, she did almost explode. The assistant manageress of a well-known retail and shopping centre, she arrived through the door of the premises and was greeted by several smiling staff who offered her big bath towels, and a few snide remarks!

I was very lucky she was working at the other end of the country at the time, as I reckon if she could have laid her hands on me at that particular moment, she would have rung my neck.

Chapter Nineteen

IN the years that followed, Eamon's capacity and ingenious ability to excite and ignite my desire for the ultimate challenge, would take me, and hundreds of other adventure and adrenaline seekers, to the four corners of the globe.

If I thought the bunch of people I met on the ski trip were crazy, they were lightweights in comparison to the next crowd I was to travel with on an entirely different challenge.

Eamon, with the help of a few close and loyal friends and the weight of the National Council for the Blind behind him, went on to create and mould a charity group, the likes of which, I believe, Ireland had never seen before and probably will never see again – The Blazing Saddles.

To give the cycling group any particular label would be impossible, but to be a member of this elite group you have to be superbly fit and boast tremendous stamina. This is not to enable you to cycle up to a hundred miles or so every day, that end of it's minor. The real stamina is required for the endless amount of sleepless nights and partying that is expected from a true blazing saddler!

I believe the age limit is from nine to ninety, and although I never noticed any nine-year-olds, I certainly questioned some of the older fellows that were a part of this notorious group. Often, to my shame and disgust, these guys would fly by on their bikes while I, with my pilot on my tandem, would be struggling to cycle up an unforgiving hill.

If that wasn't humiliating enough, on one occasion, while struggling up an endless hill, one of these geriatrics came to the assistance of my pilot and I. He literally cycled alongside us and with amazing strength and dexterity managed to push our bike up the hill by holding onto the saddle I was sitting on, with his one hand. This same guy was a show off on the dance floor and believed himself to be somewhere between Michael Flatly and John Travolta, so when he volunteered to literally lend us a hand I presumed he was doing it in jest. I reckoned he was only out to highlight our disastrous effort and the tired legs that were aching as we fought to conquer the everlasting hill.

I had to admit though, his cycling skills and strength surpassed his attempts at dancing and I was extremely grateful for this as he encouraged us up the strenuous hills that followed.

It was this unique and selfless camaraderie that made the Blazing Saddles such a brilliant organisation and one I was proud to be a part of.

It was 1993 and I was just 21 years old when I went to Florida with them. My friend and pilot at the time was an old school buddy of mine and, like me, I don't think he knew what he was signing up for when we decided to take on the Florida 500 miles challenge. Before we were to set out on the trip we also had the arduous task of trying to fundraise over five thousand pounds in order to get us there, so the challenge began right at home.

My mother was tremendous and I'm extremely grateful to her for the endless amount of hours she willingly gave to me and my mate Theo. I believe if she could have cycled the 500 miles herself, she would have done that also. The local pub in which I once worked, rallied around us too and held a race night, which was a fantastic success.

In all seriousness the fundraising was more difficult than the actual training on the tandem. Mind you, I don't think Theo would have agreed with me as I recall the mornings I called over to him and he would still be in bed. He certainly was not a morning person and it would be at least five miles or more on the road, before he would utter a word – and only then to curse me for ever getting him up. All the same I didn't mind his complaints as I remembered the long hours and early mornings a barman had to work.

It was actually Theo who replaced me in the pub I worked in, so I obliged him by listening to his rants and raves. We managed to get out twice a week, and it was not long before the two of us were fighting fit, or at least that is what we had convinced ourselves.

For those of you that have never cycled a tandem, let me give you some facts. Both cyclists have to put in the same effort, as pedals and chain move at the same momentum. Both cyclists have to have a good sense of balance for obvious reasons. It is brilliant on the flat or for going downhill, also for obvious reasons, but it is a bloody bitch when going uphill.

It took one particular incident though, to figure out exactly why it was such a bitch, on occasion. On this day Theo was suffering from a mountainous hangover and when we came to a familiar hill we both found it almost impossible to get up it.

"Are you pedalling or what?" I asked him around the halfway mark, not overly surprised we weren't doing the best.

"Pedalling?" he asked, like it was a new concept. "Sure you never told me I had to pedal as well as steer."

Only I needed his eyes to guide me home there would have been trouble.

Nevertheless, after four months of training twice a week, we managed to complete, on average, eighty miles on both days. By this time we were both convinced that if our legs were not up for the challenge that lay ahead, our backsides certainly were. We were quite proud of this achievement, because when we first started our training, both of us could not get beyond ten miles before our asses were killing us! If you were to ask any top cyclist, I guarantee you they would tell you it's the backside that gives in before the legs.

In all seriousness, we were as well prepared as we were ever going to be. Initially in our training, it was taking us almost two hours to cycle the fourteen mile from Tallaght to Blessington, but by the end of our four months training we were completing this within the hour. The incentive for Theo was that I promised him that if we achieved this within the hour the drinks were on me as soon as we arrived into Blessington. For me it was constantly nearing our goal of getting to Florida – but the pints helped!

Since the horrific disaster of 9-11, we are all aware of the extreme measures airport security undertakes for the safety of their passengers. These extreme measures, however, were certainly not enforced back in the day, as the Blazing Saddles began to board the nine-hour flight to Florida upon the famous Russian airline, Aeroflot.

I don't know if my fellow passengers were reluctant to leave loved ones behind or reluctant to leave the bar, but they were in no hurry to board the plane. It was quite noticeable that the Aeroflot crew were not in the slightest bit amused by our Irish gaiety either, and I remember being told that throughout the flight not one of the crew cracked a smile – so it soon became a challenge to make them.

Though not one bit amusing to the crew, we found it quite hilarious when one of the visually impaired called one of the staff to his side and asked her, in a very serious County Louth accent, did she ever smile?

Combined with turbulence and laughter my stomach rattled while the unfortunate hostess marched away in complete disgust; and someone else asked her if she could politely sit down as her fierce stamping was causing the plane to sway back and forth.

That nine-hour flight to Miami must have been the longest flight that crew ever had to endure, but we passed away the time with singing, drinking and telling dirty jokes.

Those of you that might have been born since 9-11, don't assume that this behaviour was common on flights before this event. I can categorically say, it certainly was not. It was just typical of the Blazing Saddles.

It's amazing the small things that I recall as I write this, in particular the blast of heat that hit us all as we finally exited Miami airport.

Out there, there seemed to be an endless amount of stretch limousines in the car park of the airport; as we piled onto our luxury coach, which thankfully was air-conditioned. The limos reminded me of watching Miami Vice on television, and I imagined that some of them were harbouring gangsters with stunning looking women.

There was no time for napping as the bus began the 240-mile route that would take us to our hotel in Orlando and the guitars were taken out for another sing-song.

Stefan Grace, who was one of the visually impaired, had written a song especially for the occasion and it went… *if you follow the Blazing Saddles clap your hands,* which went down perfectly with everybody the first time it was heard, even receiving rapturous applause – but it was slowly drilling its way into my brain after a few rounds of it. And if that wasn't bad enough you daren't not sing or clap, or you would be questioned!

I can safely state that it almost drove me bonkers by the end of the two weeks and I secretly believe it drove most of the other members half mad as well. It was actually towards the end of the trip when another visually impaired person, who shall remain nameless, plucked up the courage and said to Stefan, "Every time you sing that song I really wish I was deaf instead of blind!"

While this entertained the rest of us it his did not deter Stefan in any way and I believe he felt it his holy calling to sing that blasted song, as well as give out immaculate heart medals to everyone, on the trip. Apart from his singing though, Stefan was one of the true characters and I am glad to say he became a very close and wonderful friend of mine.

I will never forget the day that we were doing one of our lengthy cycles through the backwaters and swamps of the Everglades. After journeying for many hours without civilisation in sight we finally came across a little shop that was selling ice cream and soft drinks. Now, before I continue my story I'm sure that almost everyone in Ireland is familiar with a well-known ointment called Sudocrem, used mostly by mothers on their babies' bottoms. Well, we adults of the Blazing Saddles were also familiar with its miraculous soothing effects and healing qualities; and I can honestly state that if it wasn't for this powerful cream, my backside would literally have set ablaze on more than one occasion!

Anyway, while we stopped for the ice cream we lads also took the opportunity to apply Sudocrem to our delicate parts. The guys did not seem at all embarrassed about this, despite ladies passing in and out of the shop and often making comments from the surrounding trees.

Despite this, we got on with the task at hand and at one point, while applying cream with one hand and eating with the other, Stefan's pilot asked him did he want some cream?

I am convinced his pilot asked him just to distract him from his endless singing and with that Stefan said that he would love some. Before anyone could stop him, however, he reached out and took a huge gulp of the Sudocrem into his mouth.

He had taken a tub of ass cream for a tub of ice cream, and you can only imagine the outburst of curses and foul language that followed as the rest of us fell around the place laughing.

*

If the cycles were not tough enough in the unrelenting Florida heat, with anything from five to eight hours in the saddle, there was hardly any time for resting. As soon as a day's cycle was over, there was barely time for a quick shower before heading out again to endure one of the huge functions that were organised to celebrate our arrival in a new town or city. These functions would have the odd politician, local mayor or other type of dignitary attending, and overall, involved a lot of ass-kissing and thanking – to the point where, by the end of the night our hands would be practically raw from over applauding.

This torment we had to endure every night, and before long it became quite noticeable that many of the guys and girls, who were courageous and brave enough to leave, did so and went into the nearest bar they could find.

Apart from the few hours of ass-licking the nights were crazy and the hotels we stayed in were literally taken over by us Blazing Saddles. We Irish are known throughout the world for our ability to sing and we never let our nation's reputation down when it came to that.

On one occasion, we were singing into the early hours of the morning and it was beginning to become somewhat tiresome for the barman. His tirades were going unnoticed, until one of the lads in our group took pity on the poor fellow and commanded we all leave. We agreed, but only on the condition that the barman come with us, and we headed back to one of the bedrooms to continue our raucous singing and revelling. I do believe the poor chap did not get any sleep that night as he left the room the following morning and went straight back behind the bar, nursing a very sore head. Apart from becoming an honorary Irishman for the night and joining the gang in a sing-song, he also helped demolish a large bottle of Poitín that one of the lads managed to smuggle over from Ireland. I hadn't the heart to tell him what he was really drinking, when he commented to me the following day that the vodka he had drunk was the strongest he ever had.

*

I have many anecdotes from my travels with the Blazing Saddles and the majority of them I dare not mention as I would be sued for libel, or even worse, lynched!

There is one guy who I have to mention though, because he was one of the best characters of the Blazing Saddles. The only thing I have in common with Gerry Lenehan, I am glad to say, is that we are both visually impaired.

71

He was, without a shadow of a doubt, the entertainment on the trips, both on and off the stage. When he wasn't singing he was entertaining us with his unbelievable wit and dirty jokes.

I remember one day in particular that Gerry was sober enough to manage to get up on a bike and do a day's cycle. It was one of the hottest days and for those of us that could not read maps that well (not through blindness), the cycle route was clearly marked out by arrows that were painted on the road at varying noticeable landmarks.

As the day progressed and the sun trailed us with its unforgiving and unrelenting heat, it managed to do more than give a few of us sunstroke. It also managed to blister the tar on the road, and in doing so wiped away a lot of the painted arrows that at the early hours of the morning had been quite visible, but were suddenly practically gone. This resulted in a lot of confusion and by the end of the day there were some irate cyclists, to say the least.

Some of those that got lost ended up adding more than twenty miles to the original route, but with a lot of apologies from the coordinator and team leaders, all was soon forgiven.

It was only when the dust had settled and almost everyone was accounted for, it became clear that Gerry and his pilot were still missing. Someone suggested that both of them had probably found a bar somewhere and were waiting for the support team to go and find them – but as the hours passed the team leaders began to get more worried.

Just as a rescue team were about to go and look for the lost souls though, who should appear but the bold Gerry and his pilot?

Asked was he in a bar his simple reply was no, despite having tried his best to find one.

"Did you get lost, Gerry?" someone shouted smartly.

"Yes," he sighed.

"Did you not see the arrows, Gerry?"

And as long as I live I shall never forget his answer.

"Arrows? What fucking arrows? Sure I didn't even see the Indians."

That was Gerry in a nutshell. Only he had the capability of turning a situation of high tension into one of comedy, with a simple witty remark. He could always see the funny side of everything.

Chapter Twenty

THE following year the Blazing Saddles embarked on the group's biggest ever overseas charity trip. Over 200 of us went to Australia to take part in the challenge known as the Pacific Coast 1,000km. This cycle was, by far, the most gruelling, starting in Sydney and finishing in Brisbane.

Again, like any of the trips Eamon organised, the logistics were challenging and the day we left Dublin airport we were bombarded by the national papers as we rubbed shoulders with politicians wanting to be seen supporting such a momentous event.

Eamon never believed in doing anything in half measures, so of course he had to create a huge occasion, and how better than to have Singapore Airlines, one of the biggest airlines in the world, have one of its planes land in Dublin airport especially to ferry us all away? It really was a spectacular occasion, given the fact that it was the one and only time Singapore airlines ever flew into Dublin airport – they have not done since.

The company prides itself on its hospitality and we Irish availed of it to its fullest, while jetting across to the other side of the world in magnificent luxury. It was about seven hours into the flight when they ran out of all alcohol, and it was at that point that we knew our reputations were sealed.

Although we only stopped in Singapore for a few hours, it was somewhat of a culture shock to witness the frightening extremes of wealth and poverty that were there. We travelled by coach and one minute were blown away by the beautiful buildings and huge skyscrapers, only to find ourselves, minutes later, plummeted into the harsh reality of the slums and ghettos.

A bigger culture shock for some of the lads was the fact that a glass of beer was over seven dollars and a pint twelve! I have never known a bunch of guys anticipate a flight so much, as those that did the boarding of the Singapore flight – but for no other reason than to participate in the consumption of free beer once more.

*

When landing in Sydney airport and eventually getting through customs I assumed that sleep would be paramount… to everyone. How wrong I was! On arrival at our hotel, a dive in the pool to cool down was first on the agenda. My pilot for this trip was none other than my great mate Thomas, the same guy who accompanied me on the ski trip to Austria. He was already in Australia and was coming into Sydney late that afternoon after being up in the northern territory of Darwin, doing what the Australians refer to as a walkabout. Now, considering he had no training and had never been on a tandem before, I don't think he knew what he was letting himself in for – still though, he was prepared to cycle 1,000km with me. I don't know who was crazier, him or me, but whatever the outcome we knew we were bound to have tremendous craic along the way.

It was later that night when I got my first real taste of Australian hospitality. People of my generation would remember the famous Australian actor Paul Hogan, better known by his screen name, Crocodile Mick. Well, apart from being known for his Crocodile Dundee movies, which were all the rage at the time, he was also known for a commercial in which he was promoting an Australian beer.

So that night, while I seated myself at the bar I called to the barman and proudly asked him, in the best imitation Australian accent I could muster, for a pint of Fosters.

"Fucking tourists," he answered, and I nearly fell off my stool. "Under no circumstances do I serve that piss."

"Eh, right..." I said.

And before I could ask for anything else he slammed a pint down in front of me.

"Get that into you mate – that's a real Aussie beer, known as Victorian bitter."

I didn't dare ask how the hell they could call it a real Australian beer considering it was named after the Queen of England, but thought better of it and took a long gulp instead. I knew with this type of wit and attitude that the Australians were most likely to have a similar personality to us Irish, and in the two weeks that followed this proved to be so – to the extent that I can safely say that in some regards they are crazier.

Before going to Australia I didn't give the cycle much consideration in terms of the daily distances, and even more so the terrain. I had no idea what lay ahead and imagined the Pacific Coast to be fairly flat with some small hills thrown in here and there. How wrong I was.

The only way I can sum up the terrain is to say – "here is my head, my arse is coming." To say it made our hills back home in Ireland look like a pimple would be an understatement.

Every morning before we set out to conquer these hills-come-mountains we were briefed by our Australian coordinator on what the day's cycle had in store for us. She had our complete attention as she described the spectacular scenery we would be fortunate enough to behold and the panoramic views that the outback had to offer. She then finished up by stating that there would be a few "undulating hills" that would not be too difficult to cycle over.

The first day we took her for her word and we thought it didn't sound too bad. After all we were the famous saddlers and what were a few small hills to us lot?

UNDULATING MY ARSE! Every time she gave that description from that day forward none of us believed her, and I think some of the lads would have strung her up, but for the fact that she was quite a stunner. The females on the tour, however, still wanted to kill her.

The distance we had to cycle each day was quite long and averaged anything between 80 and 130 miles. The reason for such long distances was that a lot of the small towns we travelled through in the bush were too small and simply could not cater for so many cyclists and their support team.

The support team were invaluable, as they were the backbone of the Blazing Saddles. We cyclists had it easy as all we had to do was cycle but what went on behind the scenes was unbelievable; and at the helm, guiding the whole operation and making sure everything ran smoothly, was the big man, Eamon.

It is almost inconceivable to me how everything ran so well. Like the cycle in Florida, the backdrop for Australia was immense. The launch of the cycle is a huge event and, like Florida, the starting event for Australia was just as spectacular. In Florida, the cycle commenced from the magnificent boulevard outside of Universal Studios. The planning was as mind-boggling as it was phenomenal, and we had closed off over six lanes of traffic and had two police precincts and two fire stations guiding us. Not only that, but we had TV crews and a chopper in the air covering the whole event. For Australia we managed to stop traffic on the Sydney Harbour Bridge, while we cycled across it! Again the television crews were out in their droves.

So, the work for the support team seemed endless and they worked late into the night, long after us cyclists finished. Then they were up at the crack of dawn preparing for the long day ahead. The team consisted of bicycle mechanics, bag handlers, road support, a chef and helpers, team leaders physiotherapists and guides for the visual impaired.

The bicycle mechanics always seemed to pop up when needed on the long stretches of road. If anything they were too good and I am sure there were a few cyclists that cursed them and their efficiency in fixing their bikes and getting them on the road again.

The bag handlers were brilliant as they had the huge task of loading the bags from the hotel lobby, on and off the truck every morning and evening. Cyclists would then pick up their bags in the lobby of the next hotel, with the exception of the visually impaired whose bags would be dropped up to their rooms. It was for this reason that we lived out of our bags for the two weeks, as we would not stay any longer than two nights in the same hotel.

It's funny, but this is something I still do today – I live out of my bag for two weeks if I go on holidays. It is not out of laziness, but just a habit I picked up while on the cycle trips.

The road support team had the daunting task of making sure that the cycle ran smoothly and safely. It ensured that the roads were highlighted well. This, as I stated earlier, would usually be marked by painted arrows, but nine times out of ten there would also be a designated driver at a change in the road or at a big junction, to coordinate not just us, but the traffic as well. The support team would be in front of the cycle as well as the back, to pick up the stragglers if needed be. The team members also supplied the endless amount of water that was consumed by the cyclists.

The chef and his helpers had the task of feeding the 200 cyclists and support team every day at the lunch stops. The majority of the time these lunch stops would be in the centre of a big field around the midpoint of the cycle, and I can tell you it was a blessing to hear that the trailer and all the tables and chairs had come into view. It was there that we replenished our lost energy; and bikes and owners received any attention necessary, from mechanics and physiotherapists, to set them up for the rest of the gruelling journey.

Some of my fondest memories of the cycles were at these lunch stops, as the craic there was mighty. The banter and joking was fantastic and the Blazing Saddles' comradeship at its greatest.

Apart from our then anthem the other significant memory from those lunch stops, that I have, is the overwhelming and powerful smell of Deep Heat. For those of the cycling fraternity, this was essential for the sore and tiring legs, but by Christ did it have a knockout smell!

It was on one of these stop-offs that I met a character who I can proudly say is still one of my best mates today. There are many words I can conjure up to describe Brian, but I will use just two – intelligent messer! Also visually impaired, he has an unbelievable intellect but at the same time is the biggest joker you could ever meet.

While being interviewed live on one of the national TV stations in Australia, he was asked how seriously he trained in preparation for the enormously challenging cycle.

"Very seriously," he answered. "At least five times a week."

"Wow, you must have covered some serious mileage at that?" the presenter replied, impressed.

"Mileage?" answered Brian. "No, not at all, sure I never left the bar stool."

"What do you mean? I don't understand."

"Well, when I'm at home I favour the pint of Guinness and in fairness I'd only manage a Fosters on occasion, but knowing that I was coming to Australia I trained extra hard and am able to manage a few more… In fact, now I am capable of drinking it five nights a week."

When watching this on the evening news the Blazing Saddles confirmed Brian an honorary member, regardless of the fact he barely cycled. In their eyes he was a fully-fledged member, if not in mileage definitely in drinking capacity and spirit.

The Blazing Saddles' reputation was set in Florida, but it was sealed in the Southern Hemisphere, thanks to my mate Brian.

Chapter Twenty One

IF the torturous cycles were not challenging enough, the following year I joined another group that was affiliated to the NCBI. The charity joined forces with the well-established Richmond Brain Foundation and formed a walking group, which became known as the Terracotta Ramblers.

They were aptly named as their first major challenge took them to Asia, where they confronted one of the wonders of the world – the legendary Great Wall of China. The first emperor of China, Qin Shi Huang who was obsessed with immortality, had over 7,000 warriors crafted from terracotta so as to protect him in the afterlife. I like to think he was immortalised and reborn in the form of the big man, Eamon. Unlike the legendary emperor though, Eamon didn't have thousands of magnificently sculpted soldiers preparing to go into battle for him, but he had something much better. He had hundreds of loyal Terracotta Ramblers who were prepared to battle and conquer any challenge, on any mountain, between the four corners of the globe.

Unfortunately I had not yet joined the group when the ramblers went to China, but for subsequent adventures I ensured my place and was honoured to count myself among them. Through this group there were times I felt I had found what that great Chinese emperor spent his life looking for. Whether it was reaching the summit of Mount Kilimanjaro, or one of the many mountains of the Himalayas, I often experienced moments of feeling immortal. At the top of these mystical and spiritual mountains I would feel more alive and at one with God, than ever. I know I found the true meaning of life there, as my heart and soul soared into the heavens while climbing these majestic mountains.

In the few years since losing my sight, I had faced many emotional challenges, but these physical challenges were something else. They were a healthy distraction to say the least and they nourished my depleted heart and soul. I reckoned if I could contend with sudden blindness and all the lousy baggage that came with it, I could easily manage any physical challenge that Eamon might throw my way – and I was right.

It all started when I received a call, while I was studying in Great Britain, from none other than Eamon declaring that he would like for me to make my way up to Scotland the following weekend – to climb Ben Nevis. As I said previously, Eamon had a gift for convincing people to do just about anything.

So, at short notice I convinced my college buddy Bruce, who happened to be Scottish, to drive myself and Libby over seven hundred miles from Hereford in England right up to the Highlands of Scotland.

It was late on the first night when we finally arrived at our hotel, just in time to gatecrash one of Eamon's dramatic and inspiring speeches. As I walked in he obviously saw me from the corner of his eye and announced my arrival to the crowd present. He then proceeded to tell everyone of my long travel and determination to be with them on their climb up Ben Nevis, and stated that it was this same "sheer determination that would no doubt see me climb to the top of Mount Kilimanjaro."

He went on to say that in climbing this mountain I would be the first blind man to ever climb and reach the summit. With his speech finally over I could feel everyone looking at me in total surprise before bursting into rapturous applause. In fact, Eamon's speech was so good I almost gave myself a round of applause. He made it sound as though I could do this trek with my eyes closed – if you excuse the pun.

If people where surprised to see me there, and further surprised by the fact that I was going to climb Mount Kilimanjaro, there was no one more surprised than I was. It was more or less decided for me that I would be heading to Africa and about seven or eight pints later I had even convinced myself.

Ben Nevis was my first serious climb and in parts it was quite challenging. After finishing it though, I was quite pleased with myself, knowing that I had just reached the summit of the highest mountain in the British Isles. My euphoria was short-lived, however, as later that evening our guest speaker gave it to us straight about what lay ahead in climbing the highest mountain in Africa.

This same climber had reached the summit of Everest, so when he talked I presumed he knew his stuff. Apart from describing the physical torment we were likely to face, he said many of us would more than likely end up suffering the symptoms of acute mountain sickness, and some could even develop Pulmonary Oedema better known as HAPE, or High Altitude Pulmonary Oedema. If this was not bad enough he said that in severe cases a person could develop HACE, or High Altitude Cerebral Edema. Not trying to scare us, he mentioned that the symptoms of acute mountain sickness were a constant throbbing of the head, vomiting, nausea and extreme fatigue. He listed them off like a shopping list!

For fuck's sake I thought, *as if the others mentioned weren't bad enough.*

I'm not going to go into much detail and give the technical or medical terminology of what happens to the body in developing either Pulmonary or Cerebral Oedema, but suffice to say I concluded you're simply fucked if you get either. Listening to the graphic description of these potentially fatal symptoms, I could not help but feel a little bit paranoid, and with the influence of the litres of alcohol I had consumed, I reckoned I would get the whole shagging lot. Sitting with my fellow ramblers, the enormity of what I had agreed to do began to sink in and the realisation was scary, but at the same time morbidly fascinating and exciting.

It suddenly dawned on me that these Terracotta Ramblers were even crazier than the Blazing Saddles.

*

The best moments in life are the ones that are not planned and my decision to go to Africa the first time around, was certainly spontaneous. It was while having a few beers in my local, that my mate Tom and I came up with the idea. We were talking about my 21st birthday party and out of the blue I said, "to hell with the party, let's go to Africa." Tom had never been out of Ireland before and little did we know, we were about to embark on the trip of a lifetime.

There is something about the continent of Africa and Kenya that will live in my heart and mind forever. From the first time I was there, the landscape and people laid claim to a huge chunk of my heart, because since losing my sight it was the first place I didn't feel at a disadvantage because of that. Kenya awakened my other senses so much that it didn't matter that I could not see. I had never given reincarnation much thought but when I got off the plane in Mao International Airport in Mombasa, I had an uncanny feeling of déjà vu. Setting foot on Kenyan soil was a powerful moment and it genuinely felt as though I had been there before.

The African sun is like no other – it seemed to penetrate right through our light clothing to our very bones. Maybe it's because it was my first real adventure, but the sounds and smells are still vivid as I recollect that fascinating journey through the streets of Mombasa and onto the dusty roads that took us to the biggest national park in Kenya. It was approximately four hours before we reached the Bachuma Gate and the entrance to Tsavo National Park. From there it took the four-wheel drive at least another two hours before we finally reached our destination – the campsite where we stayed for the night. I am positive we would have made the last leg of the journey in less time if it wasn't for the amount of times we stopped to view the spectacular wildlife that casually roamed across the vast savannah, oblivious to us.

It was late evening by the time we reached the site, and I was grateful that the sun's strength had weakened by the time we began to pitch our tents. The excitement around the camp was palpable, and there was no one more excited than me, as with every passing minute I fell more in love the place. I can't recall a time that ten tents were pitched so quickly, but we were on a promise for a highly-anticipated late evening game drive. Apart from the safari crew there were fourteen other wildlife enthusiasts with trigger-happy fingers, ready to take a shot of the "big five" on their cameras. When comparing photography equipment, my mate Tom's was a peashooter compared to their rocket launchers!

I was fortunate enough to have, years previously, been introduced, to the wonderful world of wildlife by the marvellous David Attenborough, who captured and brought to our TV screens, scenes of pure amazement, every Saturday morning. The memories of those magnificent and exotic animals will be forever imprinted on my brain, and while on safari this really helped. I am not going to lie and tell you that with our guide's amazing descriptions and my memory it compensated for me not seeing the wonderful creatures in front of me, but to be in their presence, in their natural habitat, was better than any lousy enclosed zoo.

The Leopard is probably the most elusive of the big five and the Elephant was by far the most popular in Tsavo, as large herds of them roamed in the huge grasslands. To behold these huge graceful creatures was a dream come true for me and it was astonishing to hear how protective the whole herd was, when it came to their young calf's safety against predators. I think they embody everything we humans aspire to be. They are larger than life, yet have an inner stillness and tranquillity. They also seem to possess knowledge unequalled by any other animal I know.

So fascinated was I by the journey, that it only seemed like seconds before the African sun literally dropped out of the sky and darkness loomed over the savannah, bringing a frost to the air that was most definitely unexpected. After our meal, which was absolutely fabulous, our guides lit a bonfire and we all sat around getting to know each other better. As the night progressed the beer was passed around, tongues began to loosen and the staff even joined in and told us fascinating tales of previous safari adventures. Tom and I could not let a good night pass without a good old-fashioned sing-song, and only then was the night complete. I remember sitting by that bonfire, under that magnificent African sky, never having felt so alive, or happy, in my life.

*

One of the highlights of my safari was going to a Maasai village. As a child I had a fascination with the Native American Indian. They were my heroes – cowboys I found boring. And while my mates preferred to play the character of Wild Bill Hickok, I chose the wild Indian brave. Though not Indian braves, to me the Maasai were the next best thing, and so what if they were on different continents?! That's just geography – to me these warriors possessed all the same great attributes as the Indian braves of my childhood. Their cultures were similar in so many ways, as they defied the laws of the white man – determined to be governed only by their own laws and way of life. They were both extremely brave as each faced constant death and danger. OK the Maasai didn't have cowboys to confront, but then again the American Indian didn't have the danger and harassment of stalking lions on a constant basis either.

There was one tradition that the Kenyan government was trying to outlaw and that was the tradition that the Maasai held most sacred. This was when a boy was making his passage into manhood, he must face and kill a wild Lion with nothing but a spear. I want to categorically state that I deplore any kind of killing of a wild animal; but when you compare how brave the supposedly great hunters of legend were, and how they would skulk behind a bush or up a tree and shoot from a great distance with a powerful rifle, I am sure you will agree with me when I say that there is no comparison. These same clowns decimated the great herds and prides of Africa just so they could put the head of one of these magnificent creatures on their wall, as a reminder of how brave they were. What a bloody joke.

So when I was in the presence of these Maasai warriors, I was humbled, privileged and in absolute awe. And while I knew of their bravery, I never realised the tremendous sense of humour they had – but I found out fairly quickly and at no one else's expense but my own.

There are many things man has resorted to doing in order to survive in the environment in which he lives. With this in mind, the Maasai have adopted one ritual in particular, and that is the drinking of cows' blood with milk.

While totally engrossed in our guide's explanation of the ritual dances the Maasai were performing, the Chieftain of the village approached me and offered me a taste of their home-made delicacy. When my guide informed me of what it was, I graciously declined the generous hospitality, stating I had an upset stomach.

"You should take it," my guide said. "It will make you feel better."

"No thanks, I will be fine," I insisted.

"It will give you great strength – there are great powers in it."

"Honestly, no thanks." I was beginning to feel under pressure.

Then my mate Tom spoke up.

"Rob, seriously. Under no circumstances should you be refusing it. You are really insulting these people. You know that Chieftain has a big spear and all the villagers, including the children, are looking at you in anticipation... I don't like it."

I didn't know what to say, but Tom sounded so panicked I didn't want to put us in danger.

"Go on, don't be such a baby," he pleaded.

Myself and Tom in an oasis in Kenya

Getting to grips with a Tiger

Another of my past Guide Dogs, Flurry and me

Myself and Rosemary on the final stretch of the blue run – Austria

Myself and my instructor coming through the final flag after skiing down for the final of Grand Slalom

Scaling the slopes

A nasty bruise I got training in Kilternan before heading to Austria

A well-deserved break with Donal and Derek

Schirennen
Lermoos 1998

Everest

Team pics from Everest

Myself and a friend

At home in Tallaght

Products of my woodturning

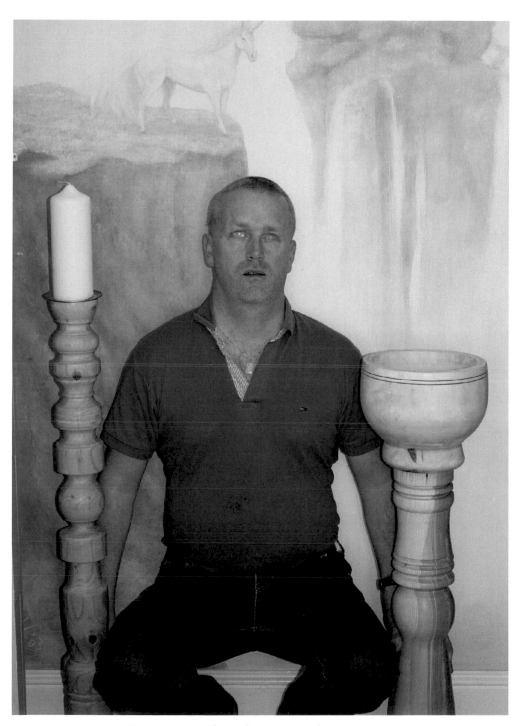

I use my wood products in my therapy room

Myself and my current Guide Dog, Ace

It was the final push I needed and so, with tears in my eyes, I slowly began to put the foul liquid to my lips, and sip from the wooden cup.

As I raised the cup the whole village began to chant in anticipation.

"You like?" asked my guide. But my mind was too full of images of discoloured blood and thoughts of the unmentionable diseases I was going to get, that I couldn't answer immediately.

As I took the first swallow there was a sudden hush and after the first sip I relaxed a little.

"This doesn't taste too bad," I eventually said, before taking another. Within seconds, however, I followed it up with, "You shower of miserable bastards!"

As I took the last sip of what turned out to be a lovely cup of orange juice, I was momentarily maddened with embarrassment and just short of throwing it over the chieftain, my guide and my so-called mate.

It seemed the whole village, including the children, broke into simultaneous laughter and it took quite a while to realise that the whole village was in on the prank. In that same moment, the Chieftain took me by the shoulders and, through his laughter, spoke rapidly in Swahili.

"Do I really want to know what he just said?" I asked my guide.

"The Chieftain said you are a brave man – almost a warrior, of strong heart," was his answer.

I have to admit I was overcome with happiness at these words, and a huge grin spread across my face as the children gathered around me in a cloud of acceptance. I felt I had passed their initiation with flying colours, and they were welcoming me into their beautiful and amazing world, if only for a brief time.

I came away from the village that day full of heart. Because despite their hardship and struggle the Maasai are a humorous, proud and awe-inspiring people and I knew I could learn a lot from that.

The following day we left Tsavo National Park and travelled even deeper into Maasai territory to Amboseli National Park. Again, this park is famous for spotting the big five and especially the illusive Leopard. Sadly we didn't get to see one, as it is very much a nocturnal animal, but we did get to see its close relative, the Cheetah.

Huge swamps that invite many species of birds, with the Pelican being the most popular, adorn this area and it is here that the immense herds of Elephants are overshadowed by the backdrop of the highest freestanding mountain on Earth – Mount Kilimanjaro.

As Tom and I carved our initials in the sand at the foothills of this majestic mountain little did I know that less than five years later I would be carving my way right up through its steep slopes to the summit – the first Irish blind man, ever to do so.

Chapter Twenty Two

SO there I was, just a few years later in 1996 back on the continent of Africa, but instead of flying into Mombasa airport, we flew into the capital of Kenya and Jomo Kenyatta Airport, Nairobi.

It was great to be back in such an enchanting country, but this time I was carrying a huge weight on my shoulders – and I was feeling it. The expectation, of being the first blind person ever to reach the summit of Mount Kilimanjaro, was enormous but I had convinced myself, almost into frenzy, that I was determined not to let my teammates or the NCBI down. Nobody had created this expectancy but me, and I was full of anxiety and trepidation.

The night that we arrived in the capital, all of the ramblers went out on the town for a taste of what the exotic city had to offer; but I declined as my stomach was churning with nerves, causing me to constantly vomit. Not realising, I assumed I had picked up a bug and predicted it would disappear within twenty four hours, but I was still feeling terrible the next day as we drove the long journey across the border into the neighbouring country, Tanzania.

Passing by the great Serengeti and Ngorongoro Crater, we travelled to the city of Arusha. The journey was spectacular as the ramblers got to see some of the most magnificent sights and wildlife. It is in this enormous gorge that over one million Wildebeest make their summer migration every year and because of this phenomena, the highest density of Lions have been recorded here, numbering up to sixty two in one given area.

After staying one night in Arusha, we continued to our safari camp at the edge of the Serengeti and it was at this famous campsite that the group got its first glimpse of the elusive and majestic Leopard. Though we were staying in tents, it didn't quite feel like that. Our tents were walk-in tents with all the amenities including a shower and even a flushing toilet – we could hardly believe it.

While staying on this site we were taken for a stroll across the Serengeti with a very experienced guide who was a native Maasai. He was a fountain of knowledge when it came to describing the various animals that were there and even the ones that weren't – all he needed was their leftover paw print. By the colour of the sand he could even inform us how old the print was, how many there were and even how heavy the animal was. When we came across a Lion print we were all fascinated with the great size this mighty animal's impression left in the sand and as we gathered around to compare our own footprints to the Lion's, one of the ladies in our company asked the guide, "So how many days old is this print?"

And without pausing to evaluate the question, he answered, "Not days old, quite fresh."

"How fresh?" someone else asked.

"About twenty minutes," he said.

With that we all involuntarily shuddered in unison. There were even a few expletives from us guys. On seeing our reaction our guide then said matter-of-factly, "No need to worry, I have my spear!"

*

It was later that evening, over a few pints of beer, that myself and the guys speculated on our guide's apparent bravery. We all eventually agreed he was pulling our legs and simply showing off to impress the girls, who were bags of nerves and stuck to him like glue on the trail back to camp.

That night, after clearly making an impression, the ramblers were invited by camp staff, back to their local bar. This, we found out, was a huge honour as we were the first ever white people to enter the forbidden sanctuary. I am saying nothing else about this night except that it was a most memorable one and I truly got the real rhythm, sounds and taste of Africa…

What happens on trip, stays on trip.

*

The following morning the mountain was beckoning as we travelled from our campsite to the Marangu Gate, where we began our ascent to our first hut. The drive was approximately fifty minutes and it gave us enough time to go over any last preparations we needed – as well as to nurse the hangovers that where lingering from the night before. While travelling I did wonder how I would differentiate between altitude sickness and my own hangover, should I be faced with the former.

On reaching the gate at Marangu, there was a huge contingent of local men all vying to be porters and sherpas for our trail up the mountain. There seemed to be hundreds of people milling about and the atmosphere was electric with heightened anticipation. While we signed in, I didn't envy our guides who had the task of selecting the porters who would, in turn, have the arduous task of carrying the necessary equipment – such as food, water, cooking utensils and even firewood – up the mountain. As I felt the shadow of Mount Kilimanjaro looming over me, I was as embarrassed and ashamed as I was nervous. Here I was watching the local people crying out to be picked to go up this mountain, so they could earn a few measly dollars and put bread on the table, while I was a bag of nerves.

What made me even more embarrassed was the fact that I was personally assigned *two* sherpas who would help and guide me up the mountain. My embarrassment, however, soon turned to humbleness. My two guides chose to give me their European names and when I asked them their native African names I could understand why they did – it was a convenience thing! No matter how hard I tried, I could not pronounce them. I soon found out that the majority of the porters had been given Christian names due to the various missions that would have, at one time or another, been stationed in their village to spread so-called Christian values.

Before ever setting out on the trail I was aware that Marangu Gate, at 1980metres, was at an altitude that I have never been. On arrival, however, we were informed that the first day's hiking would be quite pleasurable and would take five to six hours walking before reaching Mandara camp and the huts we would be staying in on our first night on the mountain. Our guide was true to his word and the first day's walk was nothing too tough. The terrain was easy going as the trail took us on a rainforest walk and it was here that most of Kilimanjaro's wild animals could be seen. As we entered the forest the group was met by a large troop of Baboons and their noisy screeches seemed to be taunting us – daring us to intrude and climb their sacred mountain, but at our peril. If their haunting cries were not irritating enough, to challenge the strongest of nerves, they then began to display their backsides to us, and some even tried to urinate from the treetops down upon us. This brought great laughter and cheer among the group, and the women ramblers laughed as they commented on the enormous size of the male Baboons' genitalia.

The climb was steady, as we followed a meandering stream that eventually brought us to our huts, which lay in a forest clearing at an altitude of 2,700metres or 9,000ft. In many regards the reason why the Marangu route is favoured by hikers is the fact that on this route, and this route only, there are huts. On any of the other trails the hiker has to make do with tents. On discovering our huts, however, we all agreed that tents might have been preferable as the huts were extremely basic and the rudimentary outhouses were nothing but holes in the ground that one had to squat over when doing the business. My stomach was still giving me slight problems and going to these makeshift toilets only exacerbated the problem. Mind you, the numerous amounts of rats didn't seem to mind the obnoxious odour and you could hear them quite clearly as you exposed your backside to them, over the small hole in the ground.

While walking that day the sun was quite pleasant and clothing was kept to a minimum. If anything the sun's rays, at altitude, can be quite dangerous and the risk of burning easily is quite high – as one of the girls on the team, to her severe detriment, found out. Oblivious to the warnings of observant onlookers, she had exposed her shoulders to the African sun and that night she was paying for her vanity when they became extremely burnt and blistered.

Apart from the one slight casualty the mood in the camp was good as we all sat outside our huts watching the glorious sun bid farewell for another day. The change from day to night was instantaneous. One minute we were all sitting around enjoying the last of the sun's rays and minutes later we were running for our extra layers of clothing. No sooner had the sun dropped out of the sky than the temperature dropped just as dramatically. As my mate Tony described it, it went from "a dazzling sun to a sky almost white with an endless amount of stars." It must have been a wondrous sight to behold.

As we sat and experienced the glory of Mother Nature's delicate hand, I couldn't help but be caught up in the magnitude of it all and a lump came to my throat. It was then and there that I realised the true wonder of God. So, I said a silent prayer and my anxiety evaporated as I was transported back to a little mountain in Medjugorje, where I had surrendered myself to his greater power. In remembering that amazing experience I further made a silent pact with the almighty that if he helped me to the summit I would dedicate it to my old mate, Gary.

I knew then that he was with me all the way.

*

After a night of loud snores and smelly human odours, it was an early start and the camp was buzzing with busy porters preparing breakfast as we struggled out of our sleeping bags to face yet another day. Without a shower there was no rush for facilities and that suited us guys just fine – the ladies, however, had to try and keep their modesty and cleanliness by using huge amounts of nappy wipes!

While having breakfast, the porters literally stood over us to make sure we ate everything that was put in front of us. I found out later that they had a very valid reason for doing this – to check for signs of lack of appetite. If anyone displayed any, it was assumed that it was the first signs of altitude sickness. So, to our annoyance, it was compulsory to eat everything. When the cook came around with food for the third time, however, we all protested to the laughs and smiles of our contented guides and porters.

On that second day we learned the meaning of the Swahili term *pole pole*. Translated this means *slowly slowly* and as we hiked from 9,000ft to an altitude of 12,340ft it turned out to be very important terminology. Along that day's trail, they said, it would be likely that some of us would begin to get symptoms of altitude sickness. Light-headedness and nausea were common factors at that height, so it was paramount that we walked slowly.

As we walked I was talked through the terrain, which changed from lush rainforest to moorland. The vegetation was spectacular as the magnificent giant Lobelia plant, with its beautiful violet flower, stood high and proud among the other colourful shrubs and flowers. How ironic, I thought, that that plant would grow at such high altitudes, because in herbal and homeopathic medicine it is used for many respiratory problems.

As we climbed we were literally walking through clouds, and as we rose above them the group could look back down upon the soft blanket below. It was only when someone said that we were already at a height from which people parachute out of planes, that we could actually comprehend how far we had come. It was around midday and about halfway to our next camp at Horombo, that some of the team began to feel the effects of the lack of air and my two sherpas kept repeating the critical words that soon became a mantra in all our heads, "pole pole." It was at this stage of the hike that they also took me aside and imparted the knowledge that, without, I wouldn't have made it to the next campsite.

They told me that the mistake the team was making was that members were constantly stopping, every ten minutes or so, for a rest and this was not good as it knocks the body out of rhythm – especially the heart. The advice was that I should get a slow but steady rhythm going and walk at the same pace as my breath would allow. Soon after, they said, my heart, breath and pace would synchronise into a steady flow. I immediately took on board what they were saying and it became invaluable to me. It was something I will never forget and it helped me reach the summit of many other mountains in the years that followed.

With my newly acquired skill, I reached the Horombo huts a good hour before the rest of the team and I remember greeting them as they commented on how fresh I looked. I can't explain it, but as the mountain was draining the strength from some of my teammates, I seemed to be drawing energy from it. I received a good amount of slagging as they scolded me for not telling them about the shortcut I had obviously found – the forfeit being that it was my turn to buy the rounds of beer that night at the bar. Altitude was definitely having an effect on them with not a bar in sight! But, of course, we being Irish we still managed to down a few regardless of the polite warnings from our guides.

Our third day on the mountain was to be a day of acclimatisation. The day's trek was optional, but advisable. Some of the team had a restless night due to the fact that we were packed like sardines into our confined huts – because Horombo camp was full with both ascending and descending hikers. Also during the night a few were suffering small, but concerning, symptoms of altitude sickness, so it was this day of acclimatisation that would determine whether these brave souls could continue to the summit or not. After a late breakfast, due to a well-deserved late morning call, some of the group started out very slowly, for the Mawenzi huts at 14,000ft. Though recommended, I did not go on this walk. I reckoned it was pointless, as I wasn't suffering from much more than a slight headache. So I stayed and sat around the campsite, taking in the atmosphere and gaining much-needed rest, knowing I would definitely need it for what lay in store.

The day of acclimatisation sadly didn't diminish the horrible symptoms for two of the team, as the mountain callously took its first victims. It didn't discriminate, when choosing its fallen, and age or level of fitness made no difference. It claimed our youngest and eldest, from the team. That day was the day of reckoning, and I believe we all silently wondered how many more of us the mountain would claim before the day was finally over. Before leaving our comrades, we all stood in together for one last team photo and after a few emotional hugs and tears, those who were able, departed.

One thing we were never told about altitude sickness is that it would play havoc with our emotions and it was tough leaving our comrades to descend before they had planned to, but we had to get on with it. After that, apart from the few setbacks, the team spirit was high and we got stuck into the last leg of the hike.

The going, however, was extremely tough and there was certainly no need for the guides to remind us "pole pole," at any point because at the heights we were then scaling there was little or no vegetation, just vast desert terrain. Drinking water was essential at that altitude as you can so easily dehydrate, but taking in copious amounts of it became somewhat of a dilemma for the women when needing to go to relieve themselves with scarcely anything to squat behind. As the day wore on and muscles and lungs began struggling from lack of oxygen, conversation began to sink like the spirit of the team. We were all finding it difficult to conserve the little energy we had and it got to the point where the women, when needing to go to the toilet, didn't have the energy to go off trail and look for a sheltered rock. They kept the small bit of modesty they had by waiting for the team to pass them by and hoping that no one else was on the trail.

It is said that when the ship is sinking the captain won't give in without a fight, and throughout history there have been brave men and women that have sacrificed themselves for the sake of others. Tony, our team leader, was such a person on that particular day. When we all began to struggle, it was his voice that gave us the boost of encouragement we needed and when some of the team had tears of pain in their eyes, he was there to wipe them away. Through his own gasps for breath, he began to tell dirty jokes and even sing.

Now at the best of times he is a lousy singer, so you can only imagine how bad he sounded at high altitude, but it was his indelible spirit that carried us. And when we reached Kibo hut, almost eight hours later, at over 15,000ft, we knew we wouldn't have never made it without his continuous badgering and words of encouragement.

Kibo is basically a large bunkhouse built on a plateau, and it was here that we were all cramped in together with other lunatics like ourselves. For the few hours downtime we were afforded we were advised to try and have something to eat and make any last preparations necessary before our final assault on the mountain. Those who needed headlights, that being everyone except me, made sure they were working; and then we all added additional layers of clothes before crawling into our sleeping bags, hoping for some shut-eye.

Though exhausted, sleep eluded me and the few hours waiting to begin our final furlong to the summit seemed endless. The next morning, however, inevitably arrived and before attempting the last leg my two sherpas took me aside and informed me that I would be walking ahead of the rest of the team. I was about to argue with them, it being a team effort, but then I decided against it. They were the experienced climbers, after all, and they obviously had their own reason for taking such measures. They got me that far, I reasoned, so I begrudgingly went with them, leaving my comrades trailing behind.

If I had any doubts that I would reach the summit, my sherpas certainly didn't, as both were determined that I would be the first blind person to achieve this goal. I never thought my body could endure such punishment and to try to put into words the gravity of it, I know I would not do it justice. Every muscle in my body was aching, it was crying out for oxygen and the fatigue that washed over me was indescribable.

Though Tony wasn't whispering words of encouragement in my ears, my two pals were at every faltering step, and just when I thought it couldn't get any more difficult they informed me that we were reaching the hardest part of the climb. All I wanted to do at that stage was lie down, curl up and sleep; but the closest we got to that was stopping to have a rest and some refreshments in the form of boiling hot tea. While the guys were preparing the tea I literally fell asleep while standing up and holding onto two sticks for support. Now, I know we Irish love our tea, but when I tell you that the cup of tea I received on that mountain was heavenly, I am not exaggerating.

As I soaked up the glorious drink I tried to bite into an energy bar but it was frozen solid – an angle grinder would have not penetrated it, never mind my delicate teeth – and after fifteen minutes of rest, which seemed like seconds, my sherpas gently asked me if I was ready to conquer Kilimanjaro. All I wanted to do was to run back down that blasted mountain, crawl back into a sleeping bag and sleep for at least a month. But I bravely smiled through my balaclava and with a frozen tear in one eye, turned to face the hardest challenge the mountain had to offer.

I don't know if it was altitude that was causing my delusional thoughts, but by that stage I felt I was in battle with the mountain and I refused to let its great magnificence and size intimidate me into quitting. Despite the fact that its giant shadow was undeniably daunting, I was resolute and even the hundreds of tonne of scree and shale it had thrown across its mighty chest, did not put me off.

It was on this final hurdle that I was reminded of a great song by Bruce Springsteen, *One Step Up (Two Steps Back)*, as I was at the stage where I would literally shuffle my feet, dragging them begrudgingly through the volcanic shale to take one step forward and slide two steps back. This monotonous shuffling was endless and the mountain seemed like a demonic creature sucking every ounce of energy, slowly and deliberately, from my body.

After hours of agonising determination we finally reached Gilman's Point – the first peak on the ridge of the crater. It is here climbers get their first glimpse of the huge glaciers, but more importantly the summit – Uhuru Peak. It is on this ridge that the mountain claims a vast amount of its climbers as their bodies collapse from extreme exhaustion, freezing temperatures and, of course, altitude sickness.

From the previous night's climb we had gained 1,000metres, or 3,000ft, in altitude; and although the summit seemed like a walk in the park with its ridge measuring just a few hundred feet, it still felt almost impossible, in my state of mind.

To be exact it is only 300metres from Gilman's Point to Uhuru and the summit, and yet it is said that two thirds of climbers don't go beyond this point. I was damned if I was going to be one of those – after getting that far I intended to be the tallest man on the continent of Africa, if only for a few minutes!

It was two hours later, after trudging my way through thick snow and ice, that I finally reached an altitude of 5,895metres or 19,340ft. The highest point of Mount Kilimanjaro – and the point where I could finally say, I MADE IT!

If I am really honest it was a huge relief that it was all over. I had reached the summit just in time for the rising sun and I could only imagine the spectacular views that lay in front of me; with glaciers to one side and the vast savannah, stretching out for hundreds of miles, thousands of feet below me, on the other.

My heart swelled with pride as I stood there that day. I had done it. I was the first blind man ever to reach those heights, and I'd done it for Gary. I took a moment to think of my old friend and I knew he was smiling down at me.

But a moment was all I had.

We didn't stay long on the summit, as one doesn't linger for long at that height, for obvious reasons. So, like hundreds of weary climbers before me, I went to sign my name in the large book, which stood proud, defying the extreme weather conditions. As I began to sign my name though, I couldn't help but wonder if it was just an egotistical act, for those wanting to leave solid evidence behind.

I had my own personal reasons for climbing that mountain and I had fulfilled them. So, without signing the book and laying claim to that wonderful and majestic place, I gave my two sherpas a huge hug and began walking back down the mountain with a much lighter step and a glow in my heart. It was just below Gilman's Point when I came upon my weary companions who, like me, were exhausted, but otherwise in good spirit. I had no doubt that they had Tony to thank for this as, like my two sherpas, he was determined that the mountain would not claim any more of his team.

As they stopped to hug and congratulate me, I wasn't sure if Tony was joking when he asked me if I was prepared to go back up the mountain with them, for a team photo at the summit. My euphoria was momentarily deflated and I categorically knew what my answer would be. At the same time I couldn't help but be saddened that I would not be with the rest of my team when they reached the top, to share in their wonderful achievement.

When I gave my answer – an unequivocal *no* – the rest of the team feigned disappointment. But when I informed them that they had yet to climb the hardest part, with at least six hours to go, they quickly forgot about me. I eventually got around to telling them that I was only joking, and despite previously not having the energy to talk, some of them managed to politely ask me to "fuck off!"

So, with mixed emotions I left my companions and headed back to Kibo hut for a few hours of much-needed rest. While walking back, the realisation of what I had just achieved, hit me; and as I was slipping and sliding, once more, through the vast amount of scree and shale, I could finally appreciate the enormity of what I had done. My spirits lifted again, when I reached Kibo hut I crawled into my sleeping bag, elated.

It seemed like no time at all before I was jealously woken up by the commotion of my team, returning in great spirits, despite their extreme exhaustion. Sadly for them though, there was no time for rest, only a short while to grab some refreshments. Then we had to pack up our belongings and begin our hike back down to Horombo hut. It is hard to describe the various emotions as we hiked, skipped and almost ran back down that mountain – but we displayed it in our outbursts of laughter, joking and the huge grins on our faces.

In the end, we made such great time that we all agreed to walk right back to base camp and not stop at Horombo hut after all.

*

My experience of climbing that magnificent mountain was unforgettable; and as well as the fact that I climbed it for my mate Gary, the night I arrived back in camp shall live with me forever.

Word had obviously spread among the hundreds of porters and sherpas that I had reached the summit and many of them approached me with great sincerity, congratulating me for my achievement. If their genuine warmth didn't reduce me to tears, what did pluck at my heartstrings, and opened the floodgates to my eyes, was when the entire community of guides, sherpas and porters began to sing in unison. Their singing was like nothing I had heard before. It was like a gospel choir, but with a deep resonance that can only come from an African voice.

Though they were singing in their own tongue, I knew they were paying homage to the great Mount Kilimanjaro, and it was then that I realised what that mountain meant to them.

In those moments, all my fatigue, pain and physical suffering at the hands of that mountain were worth it for their singing alone – I was absolutely privileged to have been a part of it.

Chapter Twenty Three

MY passion for hiking in altitude stemmed from my experience in Africa, but I wasn't like most hikers who do it for the sense of achievement. I had realised that I never felt so alive as when I was at these altitudes and so I didn't want to stop. Again I was privileged to experience this feeling when going to the Himalayas, a couple of years later in 1998. It was another NCBI challenge, coordinated by Eamon.

Climbing Kilimanjaro was magnificent, but the Himalayas were even more spectacular and, if anything, they were much easier to climb. Unlike Kilimanjaro, acclimatising was simpler too, as there was a lot of descending while ascending. When I say I was literally in the heavens, that is what it felt like, and although Kilimanjaro was all powerful, it was nothing compared to the strength and energy emanating from the great Himalayas.

I am not going to go into great detail about my hike up the Himalayas, just to say that I was in the same team that I climbed with in Africa, or should I say went with as I barely had the opportunity to actually climb with them! The sherpas in Nepal used the same tactics as the friends I had in Kilimanjaro, so yet again I was at the summit before my fellow companions.

I have one abiding memory that sums up that trip for me. While walking between the shadows of those mountains, on one particular day we came to a footbridge that we had no other option but to cross. A few hundred feet below us we could hear the sounds of a huge roaring river as it was ripping and tearing its way down the valley. When I say this bridge was primitive I am not exaggerating, as the planks were rotten and in parts disintegrated.

It was the first time in my life that I was actually grateful that I could not see.

Tony, who does not scare easily, was scared shitless while crossing but it became altogether extremely dangerous when one of the girls slipped through a rotten plank. If Tony hadn't been there to grab her she would have surely plummeted to her death. When we finally got to the other side of the bridge there were a lot of frail nerves and tears.

The huts, though also primitive, were much better in the Himalayas and that night when we reached them we all downed a few beers, regardless of altitude, and warnings from our guides. I remember the huts actually having a proper toilet that even flushed, and on our discovery of this we were all ecstatic. It is ridiculous to think that such a small luxury helped to ease and soothe some of the anxiety we all felt after that day.

The following day I met a Scottish lass in whom I took a keen interest and we ended up doing the remainder of the walk together. She later told me that on our initial meeting she reckoned I was a bit crazy.

While she was sitting reading a book just outside her hut, she could hear someone singing in the distance. Eventually, through the thick fog and clouds I appeared and she felt compelled to talk to me – if only to ascertain whether I was indeed slightly mad or not. I fell in love with her accent straight away but I doubt she fell in love with my singing. We were practically inseparable from that moment on and I think what truly drew us together was our deep love and passion for the Himalayas. Like me, she seemed to draw an energy and strength from that wondrous place.

It was as though we were kindred spirits. Up for a challenge and extremely independent, she was travelling the world and had just left India after travelling from the south right up to the north. I found her passion for life and travel intoxicating and we sat up into the early hours while she took me on her travels through her mind. It was the following day that I received a lot of smart remarks from my mate Tony and our guide. They both sneered at my making history by being the first blind man to climb Mount Kilimanjaro, but having topped that achievement by being "the only man in history who managed to make love at 16,000ft." I protested strongly of course, and again I protest in this book, or at least that is the story I am sticking with...

What I will say is that on the night in question it was extremely cold and we were both in our sleeping bags engrossed in conversation, when we heard a noise under the floorboards beneath us. Turning on her torchlight, my Scottish friend discovered, to her horror, that the room was full of rats. This sounds like anyone's worse nightmare and I admit it would have been mine if I were on my own. I am not saying I am grateful for the presence of the rats, but if it weren't for them she and I probably would have not tucked into the same sleeping bag that night.

On telling my friends this, they still didn't believe me – and they still don't. There is one thing I have no problem in admitting we shared though, and that was the climax we both felt in reaching the summit of our mountain at just under 18,000ft.

*

I did two more altitude walks after that. Again, I have to say that both experiences were literally breathtaking – and I don't mean the scenery. I went back to the Himalayas and trekked in the mountains of Tibet, and then a few years later I did the Machu Picchu trail in the Andes. I have been asked many times which of my trips was my favourite, but I can never give a definitive answer, because each destination captivated my heart in a variety of ways. Though I couldn't see the magnificent beauty of the Himalayas or the vast savannah of Africa, it does not mean I couldn't feel their energy; and one would have to be dead, not blind, not to be blown away by the magnitude of it all.

There is one place though, that opened up my senses more than anywhere else I have been to. It was a constant adrenaline rush and it offered up magnificent beauty, but more practically for me, amazing sounds that shall stay with me forever. This was my trip to Brazil, and my adventure through the Amazon rainforest. Unlike the gruelling challenges of the Himalayas and Mount Kilimanjaro, the Amazon adventure was more leisurely, so you can imagine how we ramblers partied and exploited literally all that Brazil had to offer.

To begin with, staying in Ariau Towers was the opportunity of a lifetime. The hotel was situated in the heart of the Amazon jungle and was literally in a treetop. The rooms were carved out of the huge trees and dividing them were gangplanks – five miles in all directions. When the river was in flood the lower rooms would be immersed in water, with a few Crocodiles and Piranhas lurking about. When arriving at the hotel by boat our first introduction to the wildlife was immediate as the mischievous Capuchin monkeys came swinging from the trees to give looks of disdain to the new arrivals. At first they were a welcome sight and their antics were amusing, but as time wore on, they became naughtier and more daring as they began to steal anything that wasn't tied down or nailed to the floor.

Some of the ladies in the group became upset and annoyed as their precious jewellery was literally snatched from around their necks or wrists. I was even sitting on the deck having a beer when one of the little brats jumped down onto the table and before I was aware of what was going on, it had dashed away with my drink! Secretly I fell in love with these little creatures and their antics, but I dared not say this aloud as they were driving most people mad. I have to say, though, I thought it downright ridiculous, when at one stage, one of the ladies made an official complaint.

Words fail me when I think back on the first night I stayed in that magnificent location. Although the sounds during the day were amazing, it was nothing compared to the sounds of the night, as the jungle came alive with an orchestra of animal noises, that were unlike any symphony I had ever heard. I quickly realised that there were billions of little, and some not so little, creatures out there and they could be heard splashing in the depths below, or crashing through the thick canopy in the near distance. I was made very aware that we were momentary guests in their dangerous and magnificent world.

I don't think there was one lady among the ramblers that did not fall for one of our jungle guides, and when I say they were the real McCoy, I am not exaggerating. Tarzan would have been a kitten compared to these fearsome lads. Their knowledge of the Amazon was staggering too, as they impressed us with the names of all the different foliage and species, as well as informing us of various medicinal properties. Some of the undergrowth was so sharp, we were told, that it would slice through a leather boot, yet these guys could walk through it quite effortlessly – in their bare feet! If that wasn't impressive enough they had something in store for us that would impress us even more, and scare the living daylights out of us, at the same time.

On one night in particular, Eamon casually informed us that we were all going crocodile hunting. We all laughed and shrugged it off as one of his jokes – until our guides came into the room and said that we were all to be split up into groups, to enable us to fit into the small boats they had moored alongside the lower decking. Most of us thought it would be lovely to go on a boat ride at night, but it soon became apparent that something else was going on. As the guides exchanged money we asked what they were up to, only to be told that they were having a wager on who would catch the biggest Crocodile.

Some of the women began to lose their reason when we started to pitch in a few quid as well; and as we piled into our little boats it suddenly dawned on me that if we caught a croc I had no idea where we were going to put it! I still remember my friend Brigid's excited voice, as she so perfectly described the night. Like me, it left her in total darkness apart from the hundreds of Fireflies that were hovering above the water.

We were silent with frightened anticipation and the only sounds that could be heard were the boats' small engines and the odd splash made by a creature coming up from the murky depths. It was Brigid's scream that shattered the silence, as everything seemed to happen all at once; and with lightning speed our guide dove into the water, before bringing up a struggling Crocodile. He then dragged it onto the boat and dropped its huge bulk right our feet. It happened so fast that I hadn't time to be in shock. Within seconds our guide had located the croc, grabbed it and immobilised it, leaving it sitting directly in front of me!

"Oh, holy Jesus!" Brigid screamed, as she dug her nails into my arm. "That fucking lunatic has just dumped a huge croc at our feet." She was hysterical.

"Don't worry," came the voice of our Crocodile hunter. "This lad is more afraid of you, than you are of him." With that I began to laugh.

"This is no time to laugh for Christ's sake," shouted Brigid, as she drove her nails even deeper into my flesh. At that point I momentarily considered that, if anything, it was she who was more likely to damage my delicate flesh, than any giant Crocodile. As I sat there, trying to be brave with the croc edging closer, and Brigid even closer than that, I reckon Karma was watching and was set to punish me for having romantic, no fuck that, dirty thoughts about Brigid.

I soon found out.

On getting back to our treehouse, it was unanimously agreed that, at almost seven feet in length, our team had caught the biggest croc. It took three strong guides to lift the creature off the boat and into one of the rooms, so it could be proudly paraded for all to see. It was apparent at that stage that the croc was, indeed, more afraid of us and our flashing cameras, as it struggled to break free from the powerful grip of the smiling men.

As the ramblers gathered around, however, there was a sudden scream and all hell broke loose. The croc, in a huge burst of strength, broke free from its captors and made its way across the floor to its potential escape. Through the pandemonium everyone ran for the nearest exit, but in doing so left yours truly behind. It has often been said that no matter where I am, my friend Tony would be by my side, like a married couple.

Well, although true most of the time, it certainly wasn't the case that night. No fucking way, it was each to their own!

All I can say is, it was a good job none of my mates were on the Titanic as everyone abandoned ship and I was the only one left in the room – with the frightened and tormented Crocodile. So I stood there, motionless as the croc pounded its way across the floor and stopped within inches of me. Beads of sweat dripped down my forehead and I could hear the anguished gasps of those outside – safe themselves, but fearful of my fate.

It was as though we had a face off. There I was, refusing to move as the croc, I assumed, considered me as a potential snack – there was nothing I could do, I was powerless.

Thankfully, however, it turned out that it wasn't me the croc was eying up, it was the door, as moments later I heard him dive off the platform and back to freedom in the dark Amazon below. When it was safe to re-enter the room the ramblers, to their embarrassment, found me still motionless in the middle of it. I was frozen to the spot.

My nerves were soon calmed with a few stiff drinks, however, and the rest of the night was spent giving Tony abuse for abandoning me. In his defence though, he said that saving me from dangerous Crocodiles was not part of his contract when signing up for the adventure and coming to Brazil.

In my defence, I retorted; "what a load of bullshit!"

To this day he is still reminded of his desertion by some of the ramblers and gets the odd slagging from time to time.

*

I suppose it is a given that when trekking through the Amazon you encounter a variety of wild animals and my friend Mike also had an embarrassing encounter that never leaves him.

While making our way through the jungle our guide came across a ten-foot Anaconda, hidden within the undergrowth. To the ladies' horror, and this guy's amazement, they decided to take it back to the treehouse for photo opportunities. It took four people to carry the snake as it was a tonne in weight. At least this creature did not struggle to escape and people commented that it looked as though it was almost smiling while the cameras were flashing. Mike, who was at the rear end of the snake, however, disagreed with this observation and reckoned it was sneering.

And the snake must have got that vibe from him, as all of a sudden it took a huge dump, which ended up all over Mike's colourful shirt and trousers. The smell of that snake's shit lingered off Mike for days – or at least that is what we told him!

Mike is the type of character that you can never tell if he is being serious or if he is joking. So when he asked one of the snake handlers if he could chop the snake up into tiny pieces and use its skin for a pair of boots, it left me wondering...

Chapter Twenty Four

LOOKING back, all of my trips with the Terracotta Ramblers were a great distraction from the reality of my life. As my new one was evolving, however, and I was adapting to a new type of independence and a feeling of belonging to the world again, I was also struggling with one other major thing – regaining the confidence to rejoin the workforce. I wanted to give my life some meaning and not just float through it without any real substance.

I found not working extremely debilitating and there were many days I stayed in bed until late in the afternoon, because I had no reason to get up and nothing to look forward to. Apart from walking my dog, I felt I had no structure in my life and there was a dark cloud hanging over me, bigger than any mountain I had previously conquered.

These days, when it comes to people with disabilities seeking employment it is a far cry from what it was twenty years ago. Back then, telephony was one of the few options open to me and despite being familiar with the saying *beggars can't be choosers*, it just didn't appeal to me. After that, computers seemed to be the only other option, as I already had some knowledge and understanding of them. So to build on that, I signed up to an intensive computer application course in Roslyn Park College, where I spent ten months learning a skill that would prove essential for me in my development of communication – but not my future career.

The course was in its infancy and besides myself and another visually impaired guy the class consisted mostly of computer programmers. Our teacher, although brilliant, showed real expertise in programming over applications and if anything it was my companion who taught me more or less everything I learnt in those few months. I am glad to say, however, that this course has progressed massively since and is now probably the best training course in the country for the visually impaired. I know a few that have done it since and they have nothing but high praise for it.

Anyway, it was around this time that I accidentally stumbled across my passion for life – the one that would steer me down yet another road and ultimately carve out the life I am living today.

Because of the complications of my accident, and having received a stomach puncture, the lining of it was severely weakened and I subsequently suffered from extreme ulcers. My ulcers were so bad that I lost over two stone, in two months, and I am sure that regardless of the intrusion when investigating for internal bleeding, the steroids and the stress alone would have given me the damn things anyway. My doctor's remedy for this was a tablet that only seemed to irritate my ulcers more and after two years of being on the medication I was getting progressively worse. In fact, my ulcers became so bad that they began to control my life. I was constantly moody, had very little energy and my stomach felt extremely acidic from early morning to late at night, with little or no reprieve.

This sentence in hell changed, however, thanks to my introduction to alternative medicine.

While feeling rather irritable one day, as I was out shopping with my mother, she suggested that I try having a massage, as it would probably relax me. Doubting that it would do anything for my stomach, I finally thought, *Why the hell not? Sure if nothing else, I might be lucky and end up getting a hot babe to massage me.* I still remember that massage as though it were yesterday, and no it was not that the masseuse was hot or that I was receiving any kind of titillation. The lady in question did, however, blow me away with her sincere warmth and empathy. She left me speechless when she simply asked me did I suffer with my stomach. I was baffled as to how she could seemingly pluck the question from thin air. But, she began to explain that she could feel various sensations through her hands, while working on my body and one of these sensations was emanating from my stomach. She said it was holding on to a lot of blocked energy and that she could literally feel the acid in it. I left the premises that day, confident that I was going to be cured of my ulcers thanks to the remedy that amazing lady had given me. In short I had to liquidise a raw potato every day and then drink the juice from it. It was vile, but it worked and within a month I was miraculously clear of my ulcers. To be free of constant pain was indescribable, as anybody who suffers from ulcers knows how debilitating they can be.

Considering that this therapy improved my quality of life so dramatically, I was determined to investigate and learn more about what alternative medicine had to offer. I knew my blindness would create some obstacles along the way, but like anything I did before, I was simply challenged by them – they never stopped me.

*

I have met many people who opposed a lot of the ideas I have had while on my journey and it was this lack of understanding and downright ignorance that drove me to prove them wrong. I was stopped by a lot of narrow-minded individuals while chasing a place on various massage courses in so-called holistic centres across Dublin, but holistic my ass! All they were seeing was a blind person, who they assumed was incapable of doing their course and so

I was rejected. I would love to name and shame some of these well-known centres but I had to learn to rise above it and my stubborn determination eventually won out when a centre, that I am proud to mention, eventually accepted me.

The Holistic Healing Centre, on Dame Street, was where I received the great tutelage that led me down the amazing path of alternative medicine – the one on which I am still walking today, and forever discovering new things about. Knowing that there would be some complications in my ability to learn massage the tutors from this centre had the compassion and foresight to meet me halfway, and together we overcame many obstacles. We arrived at a simple solution to how I would learn massage – the tutor used to demonstrate the different strokes and explain the anatomy to the class, while working on me. I was also given the opportunity to meet one of the tutors midweek to practice on a particular part of the body for any upcoming class.

It was in this centre that a whole new world opened up for me and I was given a foundation and passion for alternative medicine. After six months of tremendous guidance I then qualified as a Swedish Massage Therapist. By that point I had the basics of massage and in my naivety I assumed the world would be my oyster, so I decided to explore a similar avenue and become a physiotherapist. With this in mind, I applied to one of the most prestigious colleges in the country, and to my amazement I was literally stopped in my tracks, from pursuing my dream. I would have found it quite acceptable if the professor in question disregarded me on account of my standard of education, but to be refused purely because I was blind I just could not understand or reconcile with. Between his apologies, he explained that it would be impossible for a totally blind person to embark on the four-year degree course. This was because the technology used by the therapists, such as ultrasound machines, had changed considerably in previous years and there was no way of modifying such advanced equipment. He admitted, that there had been totally blind students in the past but by then, unfortunately, this could not be so.

I thank God that the law has now changed so that people with disabilities cannot be ostracised or discriminated against, and are afforded equal opportunity in all areas of life. It was an unfortunate situation, but yet again I looked to Great Britain, and the answer was there – at the Royal National College for the Blind, Hereford. There I went on to receive further training in various modules – ones that eventually gained me my Sports Massage Therapist qualification.

The year spent in Hereford was the hardest year of my life, and I found myself falling into a deep depression that peeled me to my inner core and left me shattered. It was there that I was faced with the biggest challenge of my life, which was finding my true self and ultimately realising that for the first time in my life I wasn't fighting a system or an ideology – I was fighting myself.

My first impression of the college was that it was fabulous. It had all the amenities and technology that a visually impaired person needed. I could not find fault with the place or any of my tutors, who were extremely accommodating. To my surprise I found that most students had some degree of sight, and in my class of twenty there was only two of us who were totally blind.

At first I loved everything there was to love about the college and even the social life was initially exciting and fun. It was only as the weeks passed that I began to notice the difference and the changes that began in me had a profound effect on my emotions. All my life I was part of the mainstream society and to me that was just normal, but as time progressed in the college I began to realise that it had a system all of its own. Worse again, certain students had an ideology all of their own that didn't belong in the world I lived in. To my horror I began to feel I was being slowly institutionalised.

I am aware, now, that these are not issues I had with the college or my fellow students but within myself, and I would not be true to myself or this book if I did not explain what I so desperately felt while living this chapter of my life.

It was here, through battling my inner conflicts that I came to the realisation of who I really was and it shaped me into the person I am today. The harsh reality of how fortunate I was when instantly losing my sight hit me and although it may sound ludicrous, I don't mean I was fortunate in losing my sight. Christ no, but when I lost my sight it was instantaneous and I did not have to endure the heartache of gradually losing it – not knowing from day to day whether it would get worse, or when I would wake up to none at all.

As I stated already, the majority of the students in the college had varying degrees of sight, and most of them were gradually losing the small amount they had. I never realised what a huge emotional weight this was for them to carry, until the subject came up one day in a career guidance class. While addressing us, the counsellor turned to me and in a sympathetic tone queried how horrific it must have been to lose my sight so tragically, and in such an instant way.

"The initial shock of losing my sight was horrific," I said. "But because it was immediate and totally gone, I had no other option but to pick up the pieces and try to get on with my life."

It was then that the discussion really opened up with the other students and it became quite revealing for me. They could all understand exactly where I was coming from; but some of them felt as though they were living in a parallel universe, being neither blind nor fully-sighted. They felt they were in limbo, and some even went on to confess they didn't know where they belonged in society. It was heartbreaking to hear them say that they felt they stood out in a crowd, that they felt they looked awkward and the general public often assumed they were drunk and sometimes mistaken for being on drugs.

They could not accept their predicament and therefore would not use a walking aid. They said that the majority of the time, they were quite mobile and could navigate their surroundings with little or no difficulty. However, on a day that the sun was too bright or to the other extreme, was dull and cloudy, they would often stumble into something or someone.

Listening to them, I could not help but feel that they were fighting a losing battle and thought if only they accepted their situation, life would be much easier for them. I came away from that discussion somewhat disillusioned by my fellow students; as I found it quite bewildering that they were prepared to endure the embarrassment of looking odd by stumbling into objects, rather than reconciling with the fact that their sight was slowly deteriorating.

It was over the following weeks that I came to realise that they were not just talking the talk, but were literally walking the walk and I could not help but notice that on nights when we would go out on the town, none of them would bring a cane. Granted, we would walk down in the late evening while it was still bright and they could navigate the terrain with little or no difficulty, but when night fell it became a totally different situation.

It's almost funny to recall the night that Libby and I had to guide three of my buddies home from the local bar, because they could see nothing but the hand in front of them. When I asked them whether or not they had a stick, each declared defensively that they would not be seen dead with one, despite the fact that my dog and I had to lead the way back to campus while the three lads linked arms, forming a train behind us. Surely that was more embarrassing for them than a harmless cane! What was quite ironic was that they would put themselves in such situations to avoid standing out in a crowd and being recognised as visually impaired – but if anything it was their inability to accept their situations that made them stand out even more.

Another thing that came to my attention was the fact that they stuck to themselves and never tried to mingle with the general public. I, on the other hand, would chat to the devil himself if I thought I would get a bit of craic, or a half decent conversation, out of him. So I would often mingle and by the end of a night out be talking to total strangers, before returning to my fellow students who hadn't budged from their seats the entire time.

In the weeks that followed a few such incidents, it became apparent to me that certain students in the college deliberately avoided me; as they would often pass me by in a corridor hoping that I would not hear them, or recognise their voice. This eventually increased to such an extreme, that I was more or less ignored by my classmates and I began to feel very isolated, naturally withdrawing and eventually falling into a deep depression.

I ended up remaining within the confines of my room, unless it was to take Libby on long walks through the local woodland. While in the depths of my depression, I was at a loss as to why many of my former friends were now suddenly, just that. The only conclusion that I could come up with was that I must have pissed one or two of them off and this obviously spread like wildfire around the campus. I began to resent the college and all it represented, but most of all I began to resent myself. I was questioning everything I was doing and had done in my life up to then, and I could not figure out what had rendered me so disliked by the other students.

It was the first time in my life I began to question where I belonged in society, if anywhere at all, as it was quite obvious that my fellow students were not willing to accept me. By then I even wondered if the sighted world would reject me. My depression progressed to such an extent that my grades weakened greatly and I even began to skip some of my classes rather than be ignored and shunned. I began to feel as though it was me against the college and that they were slowly wearing me down, dragging me under, and institutionalising me into their little world. After many nights of crying myself to sleep, the side of me that came to the fore was the usual one that comes charging out when I feel threatened. I was confrontational Robert and, as before, it was this characteristic that pulled me out of the depths.

All of a sudden I thought *to hell with them all. Who do these assholes think they are, ignoring me?* But my anger with them, I soon realised, was due to the fact that, for the first time since my blindness, I was questioning my limitations. Up to then I was riding a roller coaster with unlimited expectations, but suddenly the college and its students were grinding me to a halt.

In the weeks that followed, my self-preservation mode kicked in and I was determined to show them that I was made of stronger stuff and nothing or no one would take me under. I began going to the college gym, where I released my frustration and anger, every morning before classes. Amazingly the physical exercise cleared my head and I began to look at things a lot more rationally. I became determined to improve my grades, so I also began to study late into the evening and, for the first time in my life, I actually found myself enjoying it.

It was also around this time that I found tremendous escape from the smothering embrace of the college and its ever-enveloping claws. I became great friends with one of the caretakers there who, like me, had a great passion for trekking. So when the weekends came around we would love nothing better than to go climbing into the local mountains. It was on these walks, while talking with my pal Bruce, that I began to feel alive again and uncover my hidden feelings about the college, my fellow students and why I felt so threatened by them.

Through our numerous chats, and vast consumption of beer, he made me realise that, although blind, I was very much an individual and it was this individuality that I felt was being threatened. By attending the college I felt as though I was being categorised and that my identity was slowly being chipped away at. Unlike my fellow students, I was not willing to be seen as a blind man first and a person second. It was my endurable spirit that was battling to be recognised as the person I was before losing my sight and not someone who was being labelled because of his disability. I was battling with the world, desperate to declare that I was still the same person inside, regardless of how other people perceived me.

And so it was through a lot of reflection, that I uncovered my many unresolved issues and raw emotions – the strongest of which was anger. This anger was directed at those who could not see the real me, but the outer shell – a person who was robbed of his sight. Whether it was classmates, so-called friends or close relatives who didn't seem to have coped at all, subconsciously I was affected and had held it in for so long.

I know now that my anger towards these people, and society in general, was what is often referred to as the mirror image; and it was only when I began to let go, accept myself and start to have more compassion for the person I had evolved into, that I began to release all the anger.

I could finally see that there was a unique person inside of me, regardless of how other people perceived me, and I no longer cared what they thought. I was not going to be labelled or determined by something as small and insignificant as blindness. People choosing to see me as different, was no longer something for me to be worried about.

That was their issue, not mine...

Chapter Twenty Five

I CAME home from Britain, yet again, a stronger and more determined person – one who was also more at peace with the world, and himself. I was much more aware of my strengths and capabilities and I was determined to further the skills that I had acquired; and be accepted and treated as an equal in the profession of Physical Therapy.

Though I received tremendous training as a Sports Massage Therapist in Britain, I knew it was only a stepping stone, and if I wanted to make a career out of it, and have society take me seriously, I would have to up my skills and gain a recognised qualification. That way, no sports club or training centre could refuse me, just on the basis of my so-called disability.

I managed to enrol in a prestigious school of sports massage therapy under the guidance and tutelage of a well-known man in the field, John Sharkey. Again I found that I was to be the only blind person in the class, but with the help of John and the other tutors, I qualified with distinction within two years. Though challenging, I found those two years exhilarating, exciting and enjoyable; and that was down, in no small part, to the fact that I was working with people who treated me as an equal.

*

There have been times in my life that certain people, when meeting me for the first time, are a bit awkward, and often afraid of saying the wrong thing. I know it's cruel but I have been known to exploit these situations and in doing so be a right "bad bastard," as my mother would say. After losing my sight first my mates were very careful around me and would often say nothing at all rather than risk making a comment they thought would offend me.

I remember almost driving one of my friends to tears when he innocently asked if I had seen a certain film the previous night. Now, this would have gone totally over my head but for the fact that he became so embarrassed he began to apologise profusely. For me, it was the perfect opportunity to take the mick out of him.

In doing this our other mates, who were around to hear the exchange, took it that I was offended and began to give him a serious earbashing. I let this continue for several minutes, until my unfortunate friend was near crying, then I told them all to lighten up and cop themselves on. The earbashing consequently turned on me!

"I may have lost my sight," I said, "but I haven't lost my sense of humour!"

It was a totally different kind of awkwardness with my fellow students in sports therapy, however, when it came to the trauma of having to strip off in front of each other and keep as much modesty as possible, at the same time. This vulnerability in undressing, and any professional etiquette that came with it, was soon abandoned thanks to one of my fellow students, who I didn't know at the time but it turned out had a very similar sense of humour to me.

It was one of those days I will never forget. As previously, I volunteered to sacrifice my body to teach the class. So with thirty fellow students looking on I stripped down to my boxers with as much modesty as I could muster, while trying to wrap the towel around me and keep as much flesh in there as possible. As I lay on the plinth, the instructor began to expose my back, and also, to my slight embarrassment, the left hand side of my backside – or to be anatomically correct, my gluteus maximus. To be honest I didn't give much of a shit what it was called, all I was aware of was that my arse was exposed to thirty inquisitive students.

I put my embarrassment and the sense of paranoia that my fellow students were having a giggle at my expense, aside, however, and concentrated on the tutor's serious tone. Every once in a while my mind would wander though and I told myself to cop on… sure what is a bit of exposed ass anyway? We were mature adults…

Suddenly one of the students, a young lady who shall remain nameless, said to me; "Hey Robert, do you know your mickey is showing?"

"Whaaat?" I yelled out, my face now burning with shame.

"You're mickey, we can all see it…"

I couldn't understand it. One minute I had a small portion of my ass out, and that's fine, but suddenly everyone could see my….

It never dawned on me that it was impossible for my manhood to be showing while I was lying face down, so I continued to splutter and gasp while the whole class, including my tutor, broke into fits of giggles.

In my mortification I grabbed the towel for protection and sat straight up.

"Christ, Robert," she started again. "I don't mean that Mickey, no, not at all. I'm referring to the much more colourful one on your boxers…"

With that the class was hysterical.

"My boxers?" I stammered.

"Yes, the Mickey Mouse that is shamelessly smiling on your boxers." She confirmed with a mischievous giggle.

I was momentarily dumbfounded, a mix of embarrassment and admiration for the smart ass herself.

"I'll get you back," I eventually shouted over the raucous laughter.

And with that she lunged at me, whipped my towel off and in a sultry tone purred; "promises, promises," before whispering in my ear, "If you are *up* for the challenge, I certainly am."

With this declaration I was glad I had put the towel back around me as, let's just say, the blood was not just rushing to my face! I had finally found my match in this amazing and cheeky tormentor and from that day forth, thanks to her, the class became more relaxed. The joke had broken a tension, which some of the students previously had in my company. What remained was a new bond and distinct feeling of camaraderie.

There was finally an atmosphere of fun and craic, but we also remembered to remain professional… well, most of the time!

*

It's hard to describe how I felt when I finally qualified as a Sports Massage Therapist – the first blind one in the country.

I was more than ready to pay my taxes and contribute to the working world with great passion and gusto, but in my naivety I assumed that it would happen just by knocking on a few club doors. This, sadly, was not the case, as the majority of sports and athletic clubs, it turned out, would only recognise fully qualified chartered physiotherapists, for insurance reasons. This I could understand to some degree, but what I could not fathom was when one well-established centre refused me employment as I was "over qualified." I had been fooled into believing that I was finally over the obstacle of prejudiced bullshit, but apparently not.

Undeterred, however, I decided to set up my own practice and converted my garage into a treatment centre offering my sports massage therapy to anyone who wanted to avail of my expertise. To say, at first, it was somewhat daunting and disheartening, would be an understatement, but I was determined to achieve my goal, and without any financial backing or professional advice, I finally pulled it off.

I still remember my first appointment as though it were yesterday, and I am proud to say that the client is still a loyal one today – fifteen years later. If I had won a million pound, it would not have been nearly as wonderful as when he handed me my first ever payment for a treatment he was obviously satisfied with. Those twenty pounds meant so much to me, not because I had a penchant for shopping but because I finally felt accepted – my fight for equal opportunity (at least in my own head) won.

Clients, at first, were few and far between, and I was basing my success on numbers, until a good friend suggested that I try basing it on the quality of the treatments that I was giving, whether the client was satisfied with the therapy they were receiving and how I was getting that word out there. I soon built up a reputation as my clients turned out to be better advertising than any newspaper and as word of mouth spread my business flourished. Of course there were times over the first few years that I was tempted to throw in the towel because I was barely getting by, but it was my passion and determination that kept me going.

Surprisingly too, it turned out that my blindness, in the job, was also an advantage for some. I found this out when one girl confided in me, that although she loved my treatments, she came to me totally on the grounds that I was blind and she felt less inhibited. She was quite a big girl and was extremely body conscious, but in coming to me she was a lot more relaxed and not nearly as anxious.

Since losing my sight I'd had a constant feeling of exclusion in particular areas of society, but since I was contributing to it again, it was an immense feeling; as though I was being really recognised and accepted again for the first time since I was eighteen.

It was around this time in my life too that I was introduced to the wonderful art of yoga – something that had a profound effect on me.

I had spent years in emotional turmoil, and in truth am not fully past all of it today, but over the past two decades I have been dealing with these feelings and delicately peeling them back layer by layer. However, never in my wildest dreams did I realise that my physical body had gone through a similar trauma to my mind and it needed to be nurtured back to health, just like my psychological wellbeing.

My best friend Sheila was to blame for dragging me along to my first yoga class and I begrudgingly went because I had nothing else to do. My preconceived belief was that yoga was for women, and was just an excuse for them to do a bit of exercise, keep away the fat and meet up for a good gossip. Now that undoubtedly sounds extremely sexist, but I'm sure if you ask most guys out there what they think of yoga, they would have a similar opinion.

Unlike any form of exercise I had previously practiced, however, I was to discover that yoga would be a discipline unlike any other and it took me down a path of self-discovery, which awakened my tired body to its full potential. I know it sounds ridiculous, but even after that first night I could feel subtle changes in my body, like it was being opened up to the deep energy that lay within. I remember too, that over the following days I was a bit freaked out about the experience emotionally, as one moment I would be laughing and the next there would be tears in my eyes. I soon discovered that while the mind has unresolved issues and trapped emotions, so too has the body and the discipline of yoga was finally making me listen to it.

The changes in me were palpable. I was happier in myself and for the first time I cared about my body and began to respect it more. My diet practically changed overnight. Previously I ate to survive, but all of a sudden I began to enjoy food and experiment with it. My energy levels soared to such an extent that clients commented while I was treating them that they found tremendous heat radiating from my hands. My outlook and attitude to life in general became more positive and I began to wake up in the morning with great anticipation. I began to believe, again, that not only did I belong to society, I also had something meaningful to bring to the table.

I was not just captivated simply with the postures of yoga though, I was enchanted by its philosophy and its ideology. Now, I don't claim to being a yoga master – that would require *too* much discipline – but Sheila and I did embark on an intensive two-year, teacher-training course. I can vividly remember the gruelling weekends of posture forming and meditation, and Sheila and I would literally collapse on the train home from Cork after each session.

One thing I did learn from doing yoga was the importance of trying to get the right balance. To this day Sheila and I still teach it and it has become a huge part of my life. Not only has it changed me, but without being egotistical, I have witnessed the profound changes in my students down through the years too – both physically and emotionally – and that's a wonderful thing.

In recent years I have also started teaching students with special needs, and it is here that the benefits of yoga are most evident. Though some of the students are confined to a wheelchair, this does not limit their capability to learn yoga and if anything their determination to learn and improve posture is heightened. Without wishing to patronise, I have found it a joy and a humbling experience at times, to teach these students; because seeing how they live life to the full, without any regrets or resentment, is a lesson they constantly teach me.

And I never want to stop learning.

Over the past few years my passion for alternative medicine has grown and I've studied a number of other therapies, including Reflexology, Indian Head Massage and Cranial Sacral Therapy. I am currently studying Acupuncture and I believe that I am the only blind person in Ireland doing so.

About two years ago I was approached to give an "inspirational talk" to Leaving Cert students who were either totally blind or had sight loss to a certain degree. I refused, point blank, as I honestly believed that the organisation asking me had it all wrong.

How dare I stand up in front of these promising adolescents and patronise them by telling them what they could aspire to achieve? These young men and women were better educated than I could ever be, but more than anything they knew exactly where they wanted to go in life and were armed with all the hopes and dreams I had at their age. The flaw, as I seen it, was that these young students did not need to be inspired or told what they were capable of – it was the so-called able-bodied community that needed informing about how these young entrepreneurs could benefit them.

I told this organisation that it would be in their better interests if they informed and educated the employers in the able-bodied society, where inequality was rife due to a lack of understanding and awareness. They informed me that they had every intention of pursuing this avenue, but that it was for another day's work – that was over five years ago and this organisation has not approached me since.

This, however, is something I am extremely passionate about and if nothing else comes of this book but to educate people and show them that disability does not mean liability, then it will have been worth it.

Epilogue

SO here I am, more than twenty years after the fateful night that changed my life forever, and in writing this book I have come to the realisation that it was not that devastating after all.

I don't know if many people out there have really experienced what it is like to peel the layers of yourself, right back to your inner soul, but since starting this journey I have done just that. This book has onionised (that word may not exist in the English dictionary but I can't think of a better description) me to the very core, and I wouldn't change a thing.

As memories came flooding back to me it ripped at my subconscious tearing into my very depths. Like a hot geezer, emotions gushed to the surface. It brought about an honesty that I hope you will relate to and helped me face demons that I thought I had fought and beaten long ago.

And although it took me back to the depths of my depression it was amazingly healing as well.

I don't think I ever realised how difficult it would be getting it all down and putting it out there, but I can honestly say it's been worth every second. Because for more than twenty years I have been in the darkness – now I can finally see the light…